OXFORD
INDIA SHORT
INTRODUCTIONS

POLITICAL ECONOMY
OF REFORMS IN INDIA

The Oxford India Short
Introductions are concise,
stimulating, and accessible guides
to different aspects of India.
Combining authoritative analysis,
new ideas, and diverse perspectives,
they discuss subjects which are
topical yet enduring, as also
emerging areas of study and debate.

OXFORD
INDIA SHORT
INTRODUCTIONS

POLITICAL
ECONOMY OF
REFORMS
IN INDIA

RAHUL MUKHERJI

OXFORD
UNIVERSITY PRESS

OXFORD
UNIVERSITY PRESS

Oxford University Press is a department of the University of Oxford.
It furthers the University's objective of excellence in research, scholarship,
and education by publishing worldwide. Oxford is a registered trademark of
Oxford University Press in the UK and in certain other countries •

Published in India by
Oxford University Press
YMCA Library Building, 1 Jai Singh Road, New Delhi 110 001, India

© Oxford University Press 2014

The moral rights of the author have been asserted

First Edition published in 2014

ISBN-13: 978-0-19-808733-5
ISBN-10: 0-19-808733-0

Typeset in 11/15.6 Bembo Std
by Excellent Laser Typesetters, Pitampura, Delhi 110 034
Printed in India at G.H. Prints Pvt Ltd, New Delhi 110 020

This book is dedicated to the memory of a maker of modern India—Swami Vivekananda—who understood the interconnectedness of growth and well-being, and above all, the critical importance of global interdependence and religious harmony—in the 151st year of his birth.

Contents

Acknowledgements

I am grateful to Yong Mun Cheong, John Harriss, Sumit Ganguly, Vineeta Sinha, Tan Tai Yong, Brenda Yeoh, Prasenjit Duara, Himanshu Jha, and Gyanesh Kudaisya for their support for this project. Material from this book has been presented at the Asia Research Institute (Singapore), the Australian National University (Canberra), and the Centre for Economic and Social Studies (Hyderabad). I am grateful for comments of two anonymous reviewers and excellent editorial advice from Oxford University Press. The shortcomings belong to the author alone.

The work on this manuscript was funded by the National University of Singapore Faculty of Arts and Social Science Staff Research Support Scheme.

Acknowledgements

This project would have been impossible without the spiritual and material support of my family: Partha Nath Mukherji, Deepa Mukherji, Indra Nath Mukherji, Subhadra Mukherji, Suman Mukherji, Jayashree Mukhopadhyay, Anjali, Ayon, and Adheesh. The book is blessed by my mother (late Goparani Mukherji), grandparents (late Bijoya and Narendra Nath Mukherji), and father-in-law (late Basudeb Ghosal).

I have secured copyright permission from Taylor and Francis to use parts of 'The State, Economic Growth and Development in India', *India Review*, January–March 2009, 8(1): 81–106.

Introduction

This book details the processes of change and persistence in India's political economy. India is a relatively weak state surrounded by powerful social actors. Countries like China and Singapore are endowed with powerful states and can move more rapidly towards change. This can be quite frustrating for Indians as well as those who wish an economic engagement with India. Powerful social actors such as industrialists, rich farmers, and powerful ethnic groups often pose a challenge to political and economic change. Rent-seeking industrialists invest in rules that tilt policies and regulations in their favour. It can often be exasperating when one learns about India's crumbling infrastructure. For example, a highly indebted power sector which has almost gone bankrupt leaves a lot to be said about electricity provision in India. The country's potholed roads do not look promising for economic growth. Rich farmers benefit from subsidies that often crowd out rural investment. There is rampant corruption in the delivery of public services. India suffers from a low literacy level and is home to the world's largest number of poor people.

There is another narrative too—a narrative of change. India's growth rate, despite the global financial crisis and the slowdown, is second only to China's among the major economies of the world. And China's growth rate is dipping substantially as well. Telecom tariffs in India are among the lowest in the world and mobile telephone connections have penetrated even rural India and are benefiting the poor. India's stock market reforms have earned it substantial investment from Indian and foreign savers alike. The Reserve Bank of India (RBI) was congratulated for its handling of the global financial crisis. The airports in Delhi, Mumbai, and Bangalore present a very different picture and so does the Delhi Metro. India has a powerful Right to Information Act (RTI) which has inspired other countries towards anti-corruption legislation. It has an effective National Rural Employment Guarantee

Act (2005) and another legislation that ensures literacy for all (2009). This narrative underscores that while the forces favouring status quo remain powerful—the harbingers of change are also present in India.

Economic reforms promoting change are just as much about growth as they are about globalization and welfare. The change in India's growth trajectory is notable and so is its economic globalization. In fact, economic growth in India is the saga of deregulation, re-regulation, and globalization. It did not take policymakers a long time to understand that economic deregulation leads to re-regulation of another kind. For example, if telecom deregulation meant opening up the sector to private companies, the more pertinent question would be—under what conditions, and who will benefit more? The state could deregulate the sector in a manner where rules would kill private investment or it could do so in a manner that would create an even playing field. It could also deregulate the sector in a way that would kill competition by promoting one or two companies.

Promoting competition therefore needed effective regulation. Deregulation alone would not signal the end of rent-seeking industrialization. One example is stock market reform—where the powers of the brokers of the Bombay Stock Exchange (BSE) rather than the public sector posed a threat to promoting transparency and professionalism in the sector. Deregulation in this case required dealing with a powerful corporate interest group rather than the state. The Securities and Exchange Board of India (SEBI), which is a product of regulatory evolution, is considered an effective regulator. Another example is the stalling of a crisis in the telecommunications sector where the sanction of cheap wireless in local loop license to Reliance Infocomm could have killed the competitive potential of India's cellular industry, had the regulator and the government not stepped in to punish Reliance Infocomm in 2003.

A political economy perspective on reforms is critical because politics and institutions intervene between policies and outcomes. Old institutions and policies produce vested interests that favour a certain policy landscape. Producing change or reform is therefore not just a matter of making new investments or changing rules, it is also a function of who favour these new rules and how powerful they are. The political resistance to reforms can be understood coherently in Pranab Bardhan's *Political Economy of Development in*

India (1998), which argued that neither the industrialists, nor farmers nor the middle class professionals in India in the 1980s had an interest in economic reforms favouring greater competition and globalization. This could be the reason why India moved so gradually towards reforming its companies and engaging with trade during that decade. The story of economic institutions and policies, which favour the status quo, can be understood in terms of the relative power of these dominant classes in India.

So what accounts for economic change in India? Economic change has a great deal to do with how the government thinks. Economic crises often have the propensity to empower certain constituencies within government when the older economic policies look incapable of dealing with problems on the ground. This book highlights a tipping point model of ideational change from 1975 till 1990 which rendered deregulation and globalization appealing to policymakers. A tipping point is the culmination of a gradual evolutionary process that generates what appears to be momentous and discontinuous change. We hold that ideational changes within government were critical. To give one example, the manner in which India responded to a balance of payments crisis in 1991 by promoting deregulation and globalization, had more to do with the evolution of an internal consensus than external pressure from the International Monetary Fund (IMF) during the Gulf War when following IMF's advice became important during a severe balance of payments crisis. There was an acute financial crisis when India was left with foreign exchange that could finance only two weeks' imports in May 1991. A similar crisis in 1966 was met with a very different response when the ideological consensus within the government about economic policy was import substitution rather than economic globalization.

Economic pressure groups outside the government also matter. A few examples will clarify the power of interest groups. Take the case of India's highly competitive telecommunications sector. It is not only dominated by the private sector today, large private corporations are in the business of changing rules to benefit them. If some companies obtain undue advantages, the once purely competitive environment that benefited the consumer can easily be shattered. Chapter 1 will also elaborate why the power sector in India could not be reformed owing largely to the farmer's lobby which cannot easily be billed for electricity in many Indian states. Under such circumstances, economic solutions such as a reformed Electricity Act (2003), the unbundling of state electricity boards, and the entry of private players have come to naught. The government failed to create a market by diktat when a powerful constituency refused to pay for a service. Consequently, there has been no change in the quantum of losses in the power sector before and after the advent of economic reforms in India.

Economic pressure groups or class interests could be the reason why the Mahatma Gandhi National Rural Employment Guarantee Scheme (MGNREGS) which is quite successful in states like Andhra Pradesh and Tamil Nadu is not equally effective in poverty-stricken ones like Uttar Pradesh, Bihar, and Odisha. Could it be that in states where the government is unable to deal with the power of farmers who need to employ labourers in their fields, a programme that offers assured employment to the marginal farmer or landless labourer would be difficult to implement? Block and district-level officials would be driven by politicians supporting the larger farmers to subvert the smooth implementation of such a programme. Moreover, richer farmers would even oppose the birth of a programme such as MGNREGS.

Political economy explains why economic rules change. It also reveals a great deal about the distance between investments that policymakers make in changing policies, and the results on the ground. This distance can be explained by a variable that economists are often shy to admit—the power of the oppositional political forces. The substantial chapters in this book—on growth, globalization, and welfare deal with the politics and economics of the reforms process. The reforms considered in this book are not merely about engendering growth and engaging with the world—they are also about promoting welfare among the poorest strata of Indian society. We hold that the process of economic growth is necessary though not sufficient for engendering citizen concern favouring the poorest in India.

Chapters 1 (on growth) and 2 (on globalization) demonstrate that the saga of India's growth and globalization are deeply interconnected. The tectonic shifts towards growth and globalization-promoting policies in India occurred in tandem after 1991. The institutions of import substitution and state control largely held their sway in India till 1991. The government's policies were geared to manufacturing inefficient substitutes for imports rather than promoting exports. Economic self-sufficiency rather than trade had been the motto of Indian economic policy. It was between May and July of 1991 that the tectonic shifts favouring globalization and deregulation changed the very basis of Indian economic policies.

Chapter 2 details both the political forces favouring change and those that work against it. It highlights the importance of the strategic context in addition to the government's ideas about shaping India's globalization. The phenomenon of India's economic globalization refers to its greater integration with the global economy. It marks a change in the country's economic orientation because India had persisted largely with self-sufficient import substitution till 1991.

How did the government's views interact with the strategic context to produce different styles of global economic engagement in India? When non-alignment worked well for India till 1967 India could exploit superpower rivalry to finance the government's policy of capital-intensive import substitution. From 1967 till 1975 India's pro-USSR tilt coincided with heightened import substitution to produce an anti-globalization phase. From 1975 till 1990 the government's ideas favouring globalization and deregulation were effectively challenged by powerful domestic social actors. Moreover India's continued dependence on the USSR for security guarantees did not augur well for its economic globalization. The post-1991 period was especially auspicious for India's globalization because India embarked on a fairly aggressive strategy of globalization and deregulation after the fall of the Berlin Wall. The support of the US and its friends for India's globalization would be quite significant when there was no possibility of an Indo-USSR relationship.

India's growth and globalization notwithstanding, the country continues to house the largest number of poor people in the world. Chapter 3 (Citizenship) discusses both the obstacles that stand in the way and possibilities that look promising. We find that patronage democracy based on ethnic headcounts poses a real challenge for development, especially if parties can keep winning elections by providing symbolic benefits exclusively to a few significant caste groups. Second, pressure from slum dwellers living under abominable conditions could have produced some welfare exceptions by political parties to garner votes. Governments often overlook slums and illegal street vendors, and are unwilling to provide these poverty-stricken people with legal rights. Partha Chatterjee has opined that such a 'political society' of squatter groups could pressure the government to provide welfare within a democratic setting. We hold that both these routes have a patronage element because symbolic or real welfare is not derived as a matter of right in these cases.

Can one distinguish between populism and welfare that promotes citizenship formation in India? We believe that developmental parties which provide welfare for all are substantially different from those that make exceptions for ethnic groups or squatter groups. These parties redistribute land to tenant farmers; provide mid-day meals for all school children; gift bicycles for all school-going girls; and grant employment and wages to all needy citizens under the Mahatma Gandhi National Rural Employment Guarantee Act. The ability to target the poor rather than throw largesse at some strategic groups for political reasons makes all the difference between populism and welfare. The good news is that as India's democracy becomes more vibrant and poor people vote more self-consciously, these propensities are likely to be rewarded in political terms.

The most promising aspect of welfare is the enactment of citizenship rights in India. These constitute a change in institutional norms just like the shift from import substitution to deregulation and globalization. The Indian citizen's right to information, for example, challenged the view that government information should be privileged. Similarly, the right to employment (2005) challenged all those who could exploit workers by depressing wages. Also, the right to education (2009) challenged the old Indian view so aptly described by Myron Weiner (1990)—that the children of the poor do not deserve education. We contend that changes in these norms could also follow a tipping point model where ideas within and outside the government begin to challenge the old orthodoxy and create a consensus within government that drives change when these ideas have reached a critical mass.

This is a book about development in a chaotic democracy. Citizens in a democracy are frustrated, and many feel that India has not moved. This book demonstrates that change is gradual and frustrating because it occurs only when a range of social actors accept change. This kind of evolutionary change is different from those witnessed in many Asian countries where the state enjoyed substantially greater power over social actors. Reforms in India have produced change significant enough to take note of its drivers and to think carefully about how development occurs within a democracy.

1

Political Economy of Growth

This chapter analyses a growth path characterized as a 'tipping point transformation' that depends essentially on substantial changes in policy ideas within the government and the technocracy. India's growth does not follow the typical East Asian authoritarian path. A tipping point connotes a model of gradual change resembling an earthquake where endogenous changes over a long period can create large-scale transformation for predominantly endogenous reasons. The evolution of economic ideas from state-driven import substitution towards globalization and deregulation from the mid-1970s enabled the executive to initiate far-reaching changes in economic policies during and beyond the balance of payments (BoP) crisis of 1991. India had faced a similar shock in 1966 but responded very differently when the dominant policy ideas favoured autarky and government control. Even though ideational changes within the executive enabled it to engender substantial policy changes beyond 1991, powerful vested interests still hinder substantial growth-oriented policy reforms. This chapter elucidates both the changes that took place and obstacles that stood in its way.

The Indian state is penetrated by powerful social actors, more than many East and Southeast Asian states. Unlike China, India could neither abolish private enterprise nor could it embrace globalization with the same speed and ferocity. Complete state-driven nationalization as well as state-driven globalization would demand a powerful state, which would have much greater command over interest groups like industrialists, farmers, and trade unions. Policies favouring economic growth and development in India evolved gradually after certain ideas became prominent in policy circles after many years of cogitation. This is a model of growth driven by a relationship between the state and society, where the power of the state, even in its commanding moments, was moderated by the power of social actors.

Economic ideas held by dominant sections of the technocracy and the ideas which captured the imagination of powerful leaders mattered. Over time, these ideas also found support from powerful interest groups. To give one example, the birth of import substitution could be understood as an idea that persuaded Jawaharlal Nehru and some other members of the Congress Party who dominated the policy framework after 1955. But this very idea also appealed to sections of the industrial class over time who favoured industrial controls and protectionism.

Then how did the policy idea of economic self-sufficiency and government control undergirding many of the salient institutions of the Indian economy change, especially after 1991? A tipping point model of ideational change through a brief narration of India's economic history reveals that policy ideas get undermined over a period of time when expectations arising from certain policies are not met. Import substitution industrialization, that depended on replacing imports with home production, rather than export promotion neither produced robust industrialization and growth, nor did it lead to economic self-sufficiency. Around 1975, this sowed the seeds of economic change, which accelerated during the 1980s. The reports of the Government of India and policy changes suggested that policymakers wanted the government to withdraw from investment decisions and allow entrepreneurs to play a bigger role. At the same time, it became clear to policymakers that globalization or trade needed to be harnessed as a harbinger of growth. While the ideational milieu within the Indian technocracy was far more favourable towards giving private companies and globalization freer play, politics stood in the way.

The BoP crisis of 1991 is an important turning point—and it was not because the International Monetary Fund (IMF) came as a meteor from above at a time when India was in dire need for foreign exchange. Such exogenous short-lived meteoric impacts with long-term consequences have often been described as a critical juncture in comparative political economy. An ideational tipping point, on the other hand, is like an earthquake which occurs when endogenous changes gain momentum over a period of time and make an impact only after ideas have reached a certain critical mass or a tipping point. Seismologists cannot exactly predict an earthquake though they can guess when one would be likely within a rough time frame. This is because seismologists can ascertain when tectonic shifts have occurred substantially in a particular direction. This is the time when an earthquake becomes very likely. We find that economic change in India often follows a path similar to the earthquake model rather than the meteor model of change.

An economic earthquake was waiting to occur in 1991 because of rising fiscal deficit, a deficit in India's current account, and increased dependence on foreign banks and non-resident Indians for financing the deficit. The government had changed its mind, building on the development experience since the mid-1970s. The exogenous shock in 1991 was not any more severe than the one in 1966. The reason why India returned to economic regulation and autarky in 1966 was that the government was not convinced about the need for reform at that time. In 1991, on the other hand, the government made virtue of necessity and steered the economy towards globalization and deregulation, taking advantage of dependence on the IMF because the government had a different view about development policies than in 1966. This is because the government's own development experience since the mid-1970s had changed its mind about future economic direction favouring globalization and deregulation. The growth experience of the rest of Asia had played an important role in this story.

If the economic transition did not occur because of the IMF, was it inspired by the Indian business class? There is historical evidence to suggest that the Federation of Indian Chambers of Commerce and Industry (FICCI) opposed the reforms of 1991. The Confederation of Indian Industry (CII) was more supportive only because some within the CII understood the grave nature of the crisis and decided to work more closely with the government. The reforms of 1991 were largely driven by the government and the CII played a proactive role in helping render the adjustment sympathetic to the concerns of Indian industry. The Indian business class was therefore not the author of the reforms of 1991. Explanations that suggest that the pro-business orientation of the government drove the reforms of 1991 cannot explain why the tectonic shifts favouring globalization and deregulation occurred in July 1991.

Reforms in India sometimes do occur by conducting economic changes stealthily in the garb of continuity. Politicians often pretend that there is no

change in policy when in fact they have instituted substantial change. For example, it can be argued that the
gradual pro-business orientation of Indian economic
policies occurred partially by stealth in the 1980s. But
the substantial changes in policy that marked a clear
shift towards globalization and deregulation cannot be
understood by the politics of stealth. While this chapter proposes a political model of economic change,
the narrative leaves it for the reader to decide which
among the competing explanations best explains economic change in India.

This chapter reflects on challenges for India's growth.
It points to the fact that the single most important factor that poses a challenge for growth is effective regulation of various sectors of the economy. Many sectors
of the Indian economy were largely governed by the
state in the past. As the state opened up opportunities
for private companies, two kinds of challenges arose.
First, in the initial phase the government departments
tried hard to throttle private business by tilting the
regulatory scales in their favour. We find that private
companies were often hurt by the predatory policies
of government-owned incumbents. Second, as private
companies won regulatory conflicts over time, it was

7

found that some private companies tried to influence regulation to secure a greater share of the market. Even though regulatory evolution has produced positive results in areas like telecommunications and the stock market, the challenge is to produce independent and accountable regulators who are fairly independent from the executive and have licensing powers.

This chapter will also reflect on two other issues. First, globalization and deregulation has enabled the states to become more independent with respect to the central government. This has produced rapid growth in some states but not in others and has led to an increase in inter-state disparities. Second, even though there has been some poverty alleviation through economic reforms, this has been much less than desired. Economic reforms have also been accompanied by an increase in inequalities. The chapter on welfare will deal more exhaustively with challenges facing the welfare state in India.

India's growth rates began looking more like China's after 2003. It accelerated to over 5 per cent between 1975 and 1990 when India's domestic private sector was given greater room for manoeuvre. This was not a period when India's engagement with the global economy witnessed a significant rise. The paradigm shift in private sector and trade orientation beyond 1991 has been associated with higher rates of growth, over 6 per cent between 1991 and 2004, and over 8.5 per cent between 2003 and 2007. It is the latter figure that has drawn the attention of the world, as India became one of the fastest growing economies in the world after China. Even if we take the global financial crisis into account, India has grown at a rate greater than 7 per cent in the new millennium, which is slower only to China and more rapid than economies such as Brazil, Russia, and Singapore. This chapter explores how the surge in growth occurred and what obstacles lay in its path.

The Political Economy of Growth Beyond 1975

India's accelerated economic growth, at a rate greater than 5 per cent during the period from 1975 to 1990, needs to be understood in the context of steady private sector orientation beginning in the mid-1970s, which accelerated in the 1980s. Thoughts about private sector and trade-orientation arose in the mid-1970s. In 1975,

9

a special cabinet committee was formed for export promotion. A number of influential reports within the Government of India began arguing against the system of physical and financial controls, and the need for export promotion. The Department of Electronics set up within the Prime Minister's Office (PMO) foresaw the potential for India's exports in software even in the mid-1970s. In the early 1980s, Mrs Gandhi was attentive to China's trade-oriented growth and the inability of the Soviet system to meet even its food requirements.

It was politically tougher for Mrs Gandhi (1980–4) and her successor and son Rajiv Gandhi (1984–9) to undo the economic legacy built from the 1950s than it was for Deng to undo the legacy of Mao. Private sector-oriented liberalization entailed gradual disman-tling of controls over private enterprise. The corporate private sector was highly protectionist. Trade orienta-tion and substantial tariff liberalization could not be achieved and India's trade-to-GDP ratio remained constant between 1980 and 1990.

There was substantial opposition to economic deregulation. The Congress Party was largely opposed to private sector orientation. Indian industry had become so accustomed to licensed production within the protected home market that the auto industry even opposed the automatic expansion of its manufacturing capacity when it learned that it was being made to compete with a Maruti Suzuki—a joint venture between the Government of India and Suzuki Corporation of Japan. The Maruti Suzuki car quickly overtook the sales of India's known brands—the Ambassador and the Fiat cars, which had not upgraded their technology for decades. Indian industrialists had typically become past masters at 'briefcase politics'— which entailed bribing the government in order to secure production, import, and export licenses. Stanley Kochanek (2007) has aptly described how briefcases filled with currency notes were exchanged in return for licenses and other privileges that the government could offer.

Economic deregulation in the 1980s was quite substantial in relation to the legacy of the 1970s, despite the political opposition described above. It occurred largely because the government had changed its mind about the role of private companies in India's industrialization. A number of decisions were taken to correct the situation of what was perceived as low levels of

11

industrial productivity. First, some industrial deregulation favouring the Indian private sector was achieved.
A few sectors such as automobile parts and pharmaceuticals were released from the clutches of industrial
licensing—a practice that had come into existence in
1956. These sectors had earlier required government
permission before any private sector investment could
be made. Second, restrictions for large businesses
via the Monopolies and Restrictive Trade Practices
(MRTP) Act route were eased. It was now easier to
expand capacity or to manufacture a product similar
to a licensed one, without seeking permission from
the government. Third, Rajiv Gandhi was able to move
the telecommunications sector in the direction of private sector orientation. He initiated the corporatization
of parts of the Department of Telecommunications
(DOT) into the government-owned corporate
entity—Mahanagar Telephone Nigam Limited
(MTNL), despite vehement opposition from the
managers and workers of the DOT. The government-
funded Centre for the Development of Telematics
(CDOT) produced innovative technology for telephone switches, which was superior to the one
being produced by the public sector company Indian

Telephone Industry (ITI). CDOT switches had to contend with opposition from the ITI in order to succeed. This technology was licensed to private companies and continues to serve India's rural areas. These efforts produced impressive levels of industrial growth in the mid-to-late-1980s that were surpassed only after 2003.

Fourth, Rajiv Gandhi drew the more professional and modern Association of Indian Engineering Industry (AIEI) closer to the government. As a consequence, the erstwhile influential industrialists of FICCI who were habituated to obtaining licenses by supplying the ruling party with funds—a practice that was perfected in the 1970s, were relegated to the background. Rajiv Gandhi now consulted AIEI on important matters, provided it with access to government policy, and persuaded what was a small association to transform itself into an organization that would come to represent the larger interests of Indian industry.

Fifth, the period of domestic deregulation witnessed the emergence of the software sector as an export-oriented sector. This was aided by synergies between the Department of Electronics (DOE) and India's natural comparative advantage, which lay in its cheap english-speaking, technically competent workforce. The DOE, manned by technocrats with backgrounds similar to the new qualified middle class entrepreneurs, gradually nudged the government towards providing entrepreneurs with greater choice with respect to imports, and obtaining finance for imports essential for exports. It also provided the push to government investment in software technology parks. These parks provided Indian firms with cheap connectivity, office space, and infrastructure, and, gave a major boost to India's software exports.

Finally, the most important legacy of the Rajiv Gandhi government was the background research on economic liberalization that was carried out within the PMO, the Ministry of Commerce and Industry and the Ministry of Finance by skilled technocrats such as Montek Singh Ahluwalia, Shankar Acharya, Rakesh Mohan, and Vijay Kelkar. This effort was spurred in part by India's own policy failures, and in part by the rising growth rates in China and Southeast Asia. To give one example, Rajiv Gandhi's successor, Prime Minister V.P. Singh requested his Special Secretary, Montek Singh Ahluwalia, to write a memo on the urgent economic tasks for India if it was to approach Southeast Asian levels of development. V.P. Singh and Ahluwalia had returned from a trip to Malaysia and the former was stunningly impressed by economic progress made by Malaysia. Ahluwalia's memo of 1990, which was leaked to the press, was the blueprint of reforms that India carried out after 1991, when faced with a severe BoP crisis. This research and changes in the ideational milieu within the government formed the raison d'être for the half-hearted liberalization of the 1980s. It also prepared India ideationally to deal with the BoP crisis of 1991 in a manner that was impossible in 1966 when the ideational environment within the government was quite different.

The High Growth Trajectory: 1991–Present

It is important to note that the trade, investment, and infrastructure reforms of 1991, even though they constituted a break from the past, were largely path-dependent. Without the experience of the 1970s and the 1980s, the technocratic conviction required to break the political deadlock in favour of the status quo–bias in a moment of financial crisis would not have arisen. India could have acted in 1991 in the very same way as it did in 1966, which was retreat to reforms in a moment of crisis only to pursue state control and autarky in the long run. The reason why 1991 was different from 1966 was that this time technocratic conviction within the executive branch made a virtue of dependence on the IMF at the time of the BoP crisis, and pursued reforms that were unlikely within the context of India's political economy. This is why it is reasonable to conjecture that India had reached a tipping point in 1991.

Former Finance Minister Manmohan Singh is a distinguished economist whose doctoral dissertation at Oxford University was published by Clarendon Press in the early 1960s. At a time when most distinguished development economists were talking about the virtues of import substitution, Singh pointed out through detailed empirical analysis that export promotion was important for India's development. He had the support of an excellent technocratic team whose research and policy experience during the 1980s generated a sophisticated blueprint for reforms. Singh stated in no uncertain terms in his Budget speech in 1991 that the underlying problem was the unsustainability of government spending in the presence of low levels of productivity. The budget deficit contributed to the BoP deficit and engendered investor pessimism. Equally significant was the fact that Prime Minister Narasimha Rao was willing to stick his political neck out in favour of economic reforms. He chose his finance minister and trusted him. He understood that the end of the Cold War required a fundamental restructuring of India's internal and external economic policies.

The policy team took advantage of the crisis to deal with a powerful industrial class largely opposed to significant globalization and deregulation. Indian industry agreed to tariff reductions, devaluation, and easier entry of foreign direct investment because import substituting industry needed foreign exchange for imports of intermediate goods, and this finance could only be provided by the IMF, at a time when commercial banks and non-resident Indians had largely withdrawn their money from India. India had barely two weeks' foreign exchange and no alternative sources of funding when it approached the IMF in 1991. Indian industry's acquiescence to economic reforms were articulated and promoted effectively by

CII, which was earlier known as AIEI, described in the previous section.

The technocrats, who were largely in agreement with the IMF on the three above-mentioned issues, made virtue of necessity and pushed for far-reaching reforms in trade, industrial, and foreign investment policies in the first three reform years (1991–3), when India was accepting conditional funds from the IMF. The technocrats also begged to differ with the IMF. The fiscal deficit was allowed to grow after the first year, as government spending could not be drastically reduced in a poor country. Trade union laws could not be reformed. And market restructuring in areas such as telecommunications, stock markets, and airlines were home-grown efforts unaided by World Bank funds. Finance Minister Singh declared at the Gabriel Silver lecture at Columbia University in 1995 that India's tryst with globalization was irreversible—no matter which government came to power after the elections of 1996. This prophecy has come true.

What are the drivers of India's growth? First, industrial de-licensing after 1991 allowed private Indian companies to produce without the need for a license. To give an example, Tata Motors a company that was not permitted to manufacture cars during the regime of controls, took advantage of de-licensing and produced one of India's most popular cars—the Indica. Spurred by their success, Tata Motors purchased global brands such as Rover and Jaguar. Recently, the company also introduced the world's cheapest car—the Nano. Such possibilities could not arise during the regime of controls.

Second, devaluation of the Indian rupee quickly rendered India's software and other exports more competitive. To give just one example, India replaced Japan as Sri Lanka's largest trading partner in 1996 after a period of 60 years. Geography, exchange rates, and improved products made Indian goods such as watches, motor bicycles, cars, and trucks more competitive than their counterparts in Japan. Titan watches replaced their Japanese counterparts and the cheaper Indian Kawasaki Bajaj and Hero Honda bikes replaced the more expensive Kawasaki and Honda bikes from Japan.

Third, India's increasing competitiveness also arose as result of the competition from foreign markets. Even though India's tariffs are high by the standards of many East and Southeast Asian countries, the weighted average nominal tariff dropped dramatically from 81.4 per cent in 1991–2 to 32.9 per cent in 1995–6, and dropped to 18 per cent in 2004–5. India abolished quotas for consumer goods imports in 2001. Tariff liberalization, which was especially successful in the intermediate goods sector, reduced the prices of Indian finished products. Over time, preferential trade agreements with Singapore, Sri Lanka, Thailand, South Korea, Japan, and Association of Southeast Asian Nations (ASEAN) also spurred competitiveness.

Fourth, the legacy of the Foreign Exchange Regulation Act (FERA) (1974) was overturned after 1991. Non-debt creating investments of multinational corporations were viewed favourably after 1991. While the quantum of foreign investment increased quite rapidly in relation to the past, such investment was still insignificant when compared with China. A fundamental difference between Indian and Chinese political economies is that while China could promote foreign investments in the absence of a domestic private sector, in India's case, foreign investment needed to deal with domestic corporations to win regulatory advantages. This was not easy. Of the US$48 billion that India received between 1992 and 2002, $24 billion came via the portfolio route and $24 billion via the direct route. Foreign portfolio investment in India is the investment of foreigners in the Indian stock market through mutual funds. This entire amount could have gone to China in a single year. And foreign investment through the portfolio route that arrived in India via the stock markets went towards strengthening Indian companies.

A business lobby that supports foreign investment in India is the domestic industrialist who needs foreign capital and expertise to compete with the more cash-rich Indian companies. It was companies which were financially lesser endowed like Bharti Televentures in India's cellular mobile sector, that supported the government over increasing the foreign equity limit from 51 per cent to 74 per cent in 2006, in the anticipation of being able to compete with richer companies like Tata and Reliance.

India now attracts $25 billion a year in foreign investment after 2003. This is a substantial advance over the past even though this is less than half the amount that China attracts. The Government of India created the Foreign Investment Promotion Board and has legislated the Foreign Exchange Management Act to streamline investments. A National Investment Board has been established for easing business conditions for the investor. In September 2012 the government decided to allow 51 per cent equity in multi-brand retail; 49 per cent in civil aviation; and it was keen on attracting the same for pension funds, despite substantial political opposition. In July 2013, the government allowed 100 per cent foreign investment in sectors such as telecommunications and defense industries. The government's resolve to attract non–debt creating assets with foreign investment has increased, even though India is substantially more driven by domestic investment than China.

Last but not least, the entrepreneurial instincts of Indian business, which could take advantage of deregulation, were critical for India's growth. A significant difference between India and China is that while the Chinese economy is still largely driven by government-owned companies, the Indian economy is driven to a much greater extent by its domestic private sector. A quick glance at the list of top companies in Indian and Chinese stock markets reveals this pattern quite unambiguously. Indian private sector business houses are now successful business models that are being discussed in the leading business schools of the world.

Quite a few new Indian entrepreneurs, especially
entrepreneurs who were not born into wealth, took
advantage of regulatory changes favouring investment
in India. Sunil Mittal secured licenses for mobile operations in 1992 when cash-rich government companies,
the Tata group, and Reliance had not seen much potential in the sector. This first-mover advantage after the
sector was opened up, coupled with Mittal's excellent
entrepreneurial acumen catapulted Airtel to the position of the leading telecom service provider in India.
To take another example, persons on the Infosys Board
wanted to sell the company in 1990 when talented
entrepreneurs discovered that the return on their hard
work was rather unsubstantial. N.R. Narayanmurthy
prevailed over his colleagues at that time—and the rest
is history. What started with an initial investment of
$250 now generates revenues in excess of $7 billion.
The reforms of 1991 revolutionized the business prospects for this firm. Entrepreneurship notwithstanding,
the company's ability to purchase computers without
needing the government's permission, export competitiveness arising from the rupee devaluation, and the
abolition of the Controller of Capital issues who could
no longer decide the price of an Infosys share, were

three major policy changes that re-shaped the business environment for the firm. These cases highlight that while entrepreneurship is necessary, it is not sufficient for propelling business activity in the absence of a favourable business environment.

Sectors such as software services and business process outsourcing have won India acclaim as the back-office of the world. Americans fear themselves being 'Bangalored' when their jobs get outsourced to India. India's manufacturing sector has also begun to shape up after 2003. Pharmaceuticals, gems and jewellery, and automotive parts have emerged as leading sectors. Even though Indian manufacturing lags behind China due to logistical and regulatory bottlenecks, Indian companies are consolidating and multinationalizing their business operations, overcoming domestic bottlenecks, and capturing the international market.

The reforms of 1991 inspired entrepreneurship in the pharmaceuticals sector. Dr Murali K. Divi returned to India with a PhD in Pharmacy. In 1990 he founded Divi Laboratories—a firm that generates Rs 1000 crores in revenues. Dr Krishna M. Ella, a scientist with a PhD in molecular biology from the University of Wisconsin at Madison, set up Bharat

Biotech International, which produced the first cesium chloride-free hepatitis B vaccine after collaborating with the Indian Institute of Science in Bangalore. This company benefited from grants received from the Bill and Melinda Gates Foundation and the Centre for Disease Control in Atlanta.

Indian multinationals now have a substantial footprint, which is a far-cry from the days when India was scared of neo-colonial exploitation. The Tatas, for example, purchased the Tetley brand for $432 million and became the second largest producer of packaged tea after Unilever's Lipton. Tata consolidated the operations of Tata Steel to be christened as the Best Steel Company in the World accorded by World Steel Dynamics. Thereafter, Tata acquired the Anglo-Dutch Corus Steel for $11 billion in 2007, in the fourth largest deal in the history of the industry. The Corus acquisition was preceded by smaller acquisitions in Singapore and Thailand in 2004 and 2005, respectively. There have been substantial foreign acquisitions in sectors such as automotive parts, IT, the consumer goods sector and in the pharmaceutical sector since 2004.

Infrastructure Reforms

India reformed its telecommunications sector, airlines, stock markets, and banks. It has so far failed in reforming the power sector and has had middling success in reforming its ports and highways. What is interesting is that with the exception of the power sector, all the success stories were home grown and evolved in the context of messy democratic politics. The success stories were driven by the idea of promoting competition for the government-owned incumbents rather than by privatizing them. Often times these ideas reached a tipping point at the time of a financial crisis and bold changes were introduced thereafter.

India's telecommunications revolution driven by GSM cellular technology is truly spectacular, despite various periodic setbacks. The country has about 900 million lines with a tele-density greater than 73 lines per hundred residents. India's telecommunications boom, though more widespread in urban areas, has penetrated rural areas as well.

The DOT, housed within the Ministry of Communications, was averse to private sector competition. The PMO and the Ministry of Finance gradually persuaded the DOT to accept competition from the private sector. The promotion of competition, which was aided by the Telecom Regulatory Authority of India in 1997 and its further consolidation in 2000, was spurred by financial crises. Each time the rent-seeking behaviour of the DOT brought the private sector to its knees, the PMO moved quickly to upgrade the regulatory framework favouring private sector.

The sector faced a grave crisis when A. Raja, the telecommunications minister at that time, distributed spectrum well below the optimum rates in January 2008. The process did not follow due procedure and the minister ignored the advice of the minister of law, the finance minister, and even the prime minister. A few companies that acquired spectrum cheap re-sold it at higher prices for windfall gains. The regulator who did not possess licensing powers could not check the excesses of the telecommunications minister. This process has hurt investor sentiment in recent years. Even though the government erred in the issuance of licenses, steps were taken to correct the situation. The concerned minister was sent to the high security Tihar prison in New Delhi. And, the Supreme Court cancelled all the 122 licenses that had been distributed in a manner that reeked of rent-seeking propensities. The government implemented an auction with a one-time payment of Rs 14,000 crores, which was substantially greater than the Rs 1658 crores that the operators paid in 2008. Even though there were few takers of spectrum at this price, these moves signalled a political will to reduce rent-seeking and to promote competition.

India's stock markets were reformed via a similar dynamic. The government realized the need for a well regulated stock market in the aftermath of the BoP crisis of 1991. The stock market was viewed as an important institution for directing savings towards industrialization. Moreover, investments were to be driven by the market rather than political or personal preferences. There was an urgent need to curb the opaque and rent-seeking propensities of Indian brokers. This could be done by the computerization and reform of the payment settlement system. The brokers of the Bombay Stock Exchange (BSE) successfully resisted both till the Ministry of Finance deployed its powers to set up a new National Stock Exchange (NSE). The brokers had underestimated the competitive potential of the NSE. The success of the NSE produced reforms in the BSE. But reforms in the settlement system had to wait till the stock market scam of 2001, as this reform was resisted even by the regulator. The health of Indian companies and its stock markets make India a compelling destination for foreign institutional investors.

India's power sector is a dismal reform failure, despite the government's best efforts. Farmers considered electricity provision a right in many states and have successfully opposed a tariff. In addition, there is rampant electricity theft in the non-farm sector. To give one example, field work in Andhra Pradesh in December 2007 revealed that poor and middle-income farmers were in favour of subsidized high quality electricity rather than the poor-quality electricity provided free of cost by the Congress government of Dr Rajasekhar Reddy. Free power came only in the night and distribution companies did not invest adequately in maintenance. Consequently, there were incidents of farmers and animals being electrocuted at night.

Why did the government make such a political issue out of free electricity? Rich farmers hired labourers at night and could afford the maintenance costs that state-owned distribution companies did not provide for farmers who did not pay for electricity. Poor and middle-income farmers also opined that the government's claim of having reduced theft could be spurious because agricultural consumption had not been metered. Andhra Pradesh was reputed to have the best governed power sector in India in 2007.

Further, systematic interviews in rural Andhra Pradesh in the summer of 2009 revealed that even poorer farmers were using electric pump sets and benefitting from free electricity. Despite this, there were still a substantial number of farmers (though not a majority) who wished to use subsidized but better quality electric power. The tragedy was that the politics of populism trumped the politics of development. A progressive tariff could be used to make the commercial farmers and industrialists pay for subsidizing the poor farmer rather than giving away electricity for free. But it was politically more expedient to give it away free of cost to all farmers.

A Federal Market Economy

Economic deregulation and globalization have created a federal market economy in India. In order to understand the emerging federal market economy, we need to understand the contours of the investment architecture before 1991. At that time the Ministry of Commerce and Industry was under the central government. It issued licenses to private investors in almost every sector of the economy. This meant that even if Tata Motors wished to produce the Nano in Gujarat, it would have been impossible if the central government disallowed such a license. It could even keep Tata Motors from manufacturing cars. Also, public sector investment was an important source of garnering investment at the state-level. These two elements of the investment architecture were reinforced by the fact that domestic private and government funded investments were the substantial sources of investment at that time.

All this changed after 1991, in a number of ways. First, the central government gave up the privilege of issuing licenses to most sectors of the economy. Tata Motors could no longer be deprived the opportunity of manufacturing a car by the central government— not even the cheapest car in the world, in Gujarat. States that wanted their economies to grow, now aggressively began courting private investors at a time when public investment declined and domestic private investors, as well as foreign investors were welcomed. State governments were now on their own and needed to garner investment that would propel growth in their respective states.

This lead to a scenario that Susanne Rudolph and Lloyd Rudolph (2008) have termed 'the iconization of Chandrababu'. Chief ministers who pursued economic reforms were lionized and celebrated in the 1990s. They also enjoyed much greater autonomy with respect to the central government, owing to the above-mentioned economic reforms. For example, Chandrababu Naidu, the chief minister of Andhra Pradesh became a reform icon. He would run from pillar to post to attract high quality investment from firms like Microsoft. He would also woo the World Bank to lend to the state of Andhra Pradesh. Typically, chief ministers like Chandrababu Naidu and S.M. Krishna (Karnataka) would take pride in the fact that the US President would visit Bengaluru in advance of New Delhi, or when they gave Hyderabad a status similar to New Delhi. Most recently, when the state of West Bengal failed to successfully acquire land for Tata Motors to set up the Nano factory in Singur in

West Bengal, another reform icon, Narendra Modi, successfully directed that investment to Sanad in the state of Gujarat. Modi has institutionalized a 'Vibrant Gujarat Summit' held every year in the state. This summit attracts leading investors from the world over, despite Modi's dismal human rights record.

The emergence of the federal market economy has meant that states such as Gujarat and Maharashtra, which have attracted the most investment have also grown more rapidly. Some rapidly growing states such as Tamil Nadu and Andhra Pradesh have also reduced poverty to a greater extent than better growth performers such as Gujarat and Maharashtra. While producing growth does not automatically lead to significant poverty reduction, booming growth accompanied by increased taxation can be deployed to boost welfare expenditure. And, if that expenditure is strategically directed towards the poor, this can produce substantial poverty alleviation. The problem is that many states that are unable to attract investment like Bihar, Uttar Pradesh, and Odisha are also the most poverty-stricken ones and they carry a bulk of the citizens of India.

Challenges for Development

India's robust growth needed to involve more people. Its agriculture sector has been in decline since the mid-1990s. Its trade union laws increase the propensity of Indian industry to remain capital intensive, resulting in unemployment. Due to this, much of the employment has happened in the unorganized sector. Manufacturing industry faces substantial regulatory bottlenecks. Last but not least, human development in areas such as primary education and health leave a lot to be desired. The result is that even though there has been a decline in the number of people below the poverty line, a strategy of more inclusive growth would have achieved poverty alleviation more rapidly.

India is faced with its second agrarian crisis. The first one in the mid-1960s was largely due to the emphasis of the Second and the Third Five-Year Plans on heavy-capital intensive industrialization, and the neglect of public investment in agriculture. India corrected this bias after the late 1960s by giving agriculture its due importance and increasing investment in agricultural technology, inputs, and prices. The middle-income and rich peasants in Northern India produced the green revolution and made the country self-sufficient in food grains.

India's agricultural sector, which feeds more than 60 per cent of the population, has grown at a rate of 1.65 per cent between 1996–7 and 2004–5. This is cause for concern as it may result in a second agrarian crisis. Subsidies to the rich and middle-income farmers like free power, price supports, free water, and free fertilizers have not been reduced, but public investment, which can uplift all, has dipped. To give one example, the US$15 billion loan waiver for farmers announced in the populist Union budget of 2008–9 would not affect a majority of the marginal farmers. Eighty per cent of the marginal farmers did not access formal loans. Drought-proofing 60 million hectares of arable land with the same investment would have produced more inclusive results. Democracies have a propensity to get captured by powerful interest groups, which work to the detriment of larger developmental concerns.

The Industrial Disputes Act protects less than 10 per cent of India's workforce in a manner that makes it very difficult to retrench unionized workers. Any industrial unit employing more than 100 workers needs to seek the permission of the government before firing an employee. Such permission can be difficult to obtain. Unionized workers are largely in the public sector, and private companies try to discourage workers from being unionized. Industry adjusts to regressive labour laws by either subcontracting its commercial operations to smaller units which escape these labour laws or by increasing the capital intensity of production. Even though some state governments have been favouring employers in recent times aided by favourable verdicts by the courts, a stable contract between a worker and an employee that protects the worker in return for productive labour has yet to evolve.

Inclusive growth demands labour-intensive production, aided by rational labour laws. Labour power is required for dealing with the rapacious nature of largely unregulated industrialists who work in unison with a captured state. Manjusha Nair's research (2011) on Chhattisgarh reminds us that labour power needs to be deployed and is often effective when it challenges the industrialists but not the state in any fundamental way. Trade union power that is inclusive and well-organized by a genuinely committed and charismatic leader, can go a long way in unionizing the poor and protecting their legitimate rights. Such social movements that seek to make the state more responsive to the genuine concerns of the citizenry have either been too few or have not been well-researched.

Consequently, India's growth has made a dent on poverty, but it has happened at an alarmingly slow pace. The country's achievement with respect to redistribution, lags behind its achievement with respect to growth. There is substantial debate regarding the extent of poverty-reduction in India between 1993 and 1999. These differences are driven by the differing methodologies by which consumption data was collected in the 55th round of the National Sample Survey and earlier rounds. A reasonable guess is that the extent of poverty reduction was 7 per cent during this period, which means that 30 per cent Indians still lived below a rather austere poverty line in 1999. The most recent data published by the National Sample Survey Organization (2011–12) suggests that there has been a relatively sharp reduction in poverty in 2010–11 and 2011–12. Poverty alleviation at a time when the growth rate had dipped suggests that this could be due to welfare schemes like the National Rural Employment Guarantee Scheme that will be discussed at length in Chapter 3.

It seems that India's economic liberalization nei-ther hurt nor remarkably impacted poverty reduction. Nor did India's earlier strategy of import substitution reduce poverty, as the proportion of the absolutely of poor in India kept increasing till the 1970s. The proportion of those living below the poverty line started declining in the 1970s but the total number of absolutely poor people began to decline only after the 1980s. The number of people living on less than a dollar a day decreased marginally from 296 million to 266 million between 1981 and 2005. It is how-ever worth noting that states such as Tamil Nadu and Andhra Pradesh that attracted investments have also made a dent on poverty, whereas those such as Odisha and Chhattisgarh that failed to do so, have also been unsuccessful in reducing poverty . How the country is dealing with the crisis poverty in India is discussed at length in Chapter 3.

Economic growth is necessary for addressing the cause of the average Indian. The country needed to promote a developmental, transparent, and investor-friendly democracy. Industrial regulations in India make it more difficult to make a success of manufacturing investment in India relative to China, despite the progress made after 1991. Indian firms can invest in any sector but need state and central government permission on a variety of issues ranging from land, labour, environment, electricity, water, taxation, and many more. These regulations often become a source of rent-seeking and patronage rather than speedy and judicious clearance of an investment proposal based on its merits. India is not an easy place to begin business in manufacturing, unless one finds a willing state government taking an initiative to make a success of the investment. The process of initiating manufacturing investment needs to be made more transparent and less cumbersome. Second, Indian industry is negatively served by poor ports and roads, and is crippled by power cuts. India's airports, though, have improved in recent years.

India's industrialization is beginning to demand more and more land. Industrial land acquisition needs to be based on the consent of the local people. It needs to be preceded by compensation and welfare measures that renders the acquisition of land for industrial purposes a developmental endeavor. Fertile double-cropped land should be largely left alone for cultivation. The current laws give the government substantial powers to acquire land. Forced land acquisition by the government has led to violent unrest in some parts of India.

Land acquisition has been successful in areas where developers have worked with state governments and the local people for gaining consent by attempting to uplift their conditions. States like Tamil Nadu, Andhra Pradesh, Gujarat, Maharashtra, and Haryana have streamlined these procedures at the subnational level. Investment friendly states are able to craft developmental bureaucracies that work more effectively for the local people and investors. The government is concerned about the issue of acquisition and a new land acquisition act has been approved by the cabinet in October 2012.

The success of Indian entrepreneurship lay in the fact that it was able to overcome these bottlenecks and grow. The software sector was especially lucky because it needed roads, ports, airports, and power to a much lesser extent than manufacturing. It was aided by India's success in creating efficient telecommunications, stock markets, and the financial infrastructure.

★ ★ ★

The trajectory of economic policies favouring India's growth was path dependent. From 1947 to 1975 the policy consensus favoured an important role of the state within a relatively closed economy. Private enterprise survived during this period but India's trade declined. Changes in the policy consensus favouring economic deregulation began to appear in the mid-1970s, which prepared the ground for the tectonic policy shifts beyond 1991.

Economic change in India can be likened to an ideational tipping point. India's gradualism can be frustrating. But it works through a process by which the government changes its mind, building over decades of policy failure and experimentation. Crises often highlight these failures but what looks like a discontinuous change has an ideational past which has been building up over a long period. The reason why India responded differently to the BoP crisis in 1991 than the one in 1966 cannot be understood in terms of external pressure. It needs to be understood in terms of the dominant ideas of the day in 1966 and in 1991. India was prepared for globalization and deregulation in 1991, but not in 1966. Similarly, the policy announcements of September 2012 favouring

41

foreign investment reveal that influential sections of the government believe that foreign investment and non-debt creating assets are an important resource for India's growth. The government was willing to face substantial political opposition because it felt that this was the right way to go.

Why then has the government failed in so many areas that directly impact India's growth? These are areas where the government is unable to deal with oppositional politics. The concentrated trade union lobby has successfully stalled legislations that would make trade unions more inclusive and orientated towards productivity. India's industrialization continues to be capital and knowledge intensive at a time when over 250 million people survive on less than a dollar a day. If India grows in this way it will take longer to eradicate poverty, illiteracy, and malnutrition. This is serious challenge and the government is attempting to address it with the National Skills Development Corporation, which is a public-private partnership seeking to cash in on India's demographic dividend.

Effective, autonomous, and independent regulators are essential for checking grand corruption. Without such regulation large cash rich companies will tilt policies to favour their monopolistic propensities. Also, monopoly capitalism can be more debilitating for the consumer than inefficient public sector monopolies. India has a long way to traverse in that direction. The state and the civil society have to work in harmony to check corruption that reduces the impact of every citizen-friendly government initiative. It is important that the government be responsive to a vigilant civil society, and the civil society be more responsible in the best interests of good governance.

India's high growth trajectory, which is essential for development, has become reasonably stable. The debate is not about whether India will grow at 6 per cent or at 4 per cent per annum. The debate is whether India can grow at 8 per cent or 6 per cent, even during a global financial crisis. One forgets that less powerful exogenous shocks in the past had driven the country to bankruptcy. This is a substantial achievement. It has been achieved in the context of democratic politics, where changes in policy orientation have been slow because it is difficult to produce new winners in the economy by not causing injury to some social groups or classes. Rich farmers, unions, industrialists, and a substantial section of government officials—each favoured the status quo and thus supported a protected economy and the public sector. This coalition is gradually beginning to favour growth and competition as the middle class learns that the competition game is a rewarding one.

The challenge for India's growth and development is to get a larger proportion of the Indian people into its middle class, which is well-served by markets and competition. This enterprise demands an active role of the Indian state and will demand support from its society.

Economic change in India was more gradual than in China or East Asia. Even though India embarked on the process around the same time as China in the late 1970s, the Indian state was relatively weak in its capacity to deal with powerful political constituencies ranged against economic reforms. Over time, however, India's growth resembled China's as it became the second most rapidly growing major economy in the world. That this growth could occur in a cacophonous democracy must surely pose a puzzle for the development literature that has celebrated the relationship between an authoritarian state and economic growth. India's growth lags behind China's, but the country has greater capacity to engender growth with consent, despite the path being ridden with many pitfalls.

2

India's Economic Globalization

This chapter explains the twists and turns in India's foreign economic policies that have generated economic globalization and growth after 1991. The average tariff fell gradually from an incredibly high level of 145 per cent in 1990 to 9 per cent in 2010. India was one of the most protected economies in the world in 1990. Restrictions on inward and outward foreign investment have been eased substantially. Inward foreign investment in India which was negligible in 1990 rose to $24 billion between 1992 and 2002. The same figure exceeded $30 billion in one year (2011). Portfolio investment—the investment of foreign funds in the Indian stock market was negligible in 1990. In 2010, it accounted for 1.8 per cent of gross domestic product (GDP). The ratio of India's exports to GDP rose from 7 per cent in 1990 to 22 per cent in 2010; and its trade to GDP ratio also surged quite remarkably from 17 to 49 per cent during the same period.

The previous chapter detailed the consequences of deregulation and globalization for India's growth story. The next chapter will point to the low levels of human development despite deregulation, globalization, and economic growth in India. The problems associated with the lack of India's redistributive potential in an era of globalization lie more with domestic political economy than with the impact of globalization on the Indian economy.

Contrary to the views of a powerful political constituency ranged against India's globalization, global engagement has generated substantial benefits for the Indian economy. The previous chapter described how India was unable to weather even a minor exogenous shock when the price of oil rose during the Gulf War in 1990–1. Subsequently, the economy has been far more resilient to the Asian (1997–8) and the global financial crises (2008). In 2012, India could sustain a current account deficit of 4 per cent (greater than 1991) and a fiscal deficit of 8.5 per cent (comparable with 1991) only because investors had not given up their faith in the India's globalization and growth. Consequently India's welfare spending also depends on its strategy of attracting global investments.

The era of the East India Company syndrome is over even though lazy businessmen continue to hide behind considerable obstacles to foreign investment and competition in India. Multinational companies have strengthened Indian companies and have often promoted competition within the domestic market leading to substantial productivity gains. It is not well known that India's leading telecom company Airtel benefited from investments by Sing Tel and Warburg Pincus that empowered entrepreneurial giant Sunil Bharti Mittal to deal with competition from the more cash-rich Indian companies belonging to the Tata and Reliance group of industries. The presence of information technology giants like Microsoft, Intel, and Oracle have not rendered Indian companies such as Tata Consultancy Services, and Infosys inconsequential. General Electric has outsourced very significant research and development to its research facility in Bengaluru.

How can one understand the roots of India's post-colonial globalization? This chapter holds that both, the dominant economic ideas held within government and the strategic setting shaped India's possibilities of globalization. First, let us turn to the issue of economic ideas. If the Indian government was not convinced about exploiting trade and investment as a tool for growth and development, it would have been possible to coerce India to globalize. The idea that India would not need trade to develop was quite dominant in the 1950s. The post-colonial aftermath and the view that the East India Company and subsequently British rule had produced the economic decline of India were dominant at this time. Added to this was the powerful theory of import substituting industrialization in development economics. Influential development economists held that industrialization needed state protection and guidance for a long period of time for economies of scale and competitiveness to evolve. Moreover, economies of scale also depended on network externalities. Steel plants, for example, would need iron ore, roads, finances, and a variety of infrastructural facilities to become economically viable.

49

India therefore needed to protect steel production from foreign competition before it became internationally competitive. The import substituting argument suggested that if India left steel production to the play of market forces it would never become globally competitive in the manufacture of steel. And, to the policymaker at that time, producing steel was more important than producing cotton. Industries therefore had to be protected from competition.

A number of policy instruments were born as a consequence. First, the rupee was deliberately overvalued. An overvalued rupee rendered imports less expensive. This helped because import substitution depended on the imports of intermediate goods. Second, while cheap imports were necessary for import substitution, they had to be curbed due to foreign exchange constraints faced by the government. Imports of consumer goods and non-essential items were blocked by high tariff walls, quotas, and import bans. To give one example, Vijay Amritraj, the legendary Indian tennis star would have to pay much more than the price of the Volvo car upon winning the Volvo Tennis Tournament in the US in 1973. Third, production was encouraged within the public sector and was planned in a manner that would allow the government to utilize resources optimally. Fourth, private companies had a role but they needed licenses from the government so that the production decisions of private firms were dictated by the government's agenda of planned development.

This chapter demonstrates that these dominant economic ideas had a legacy that endured from mid-1950s through to the decade of the 1970s. The period between 1975 and 1990s was a period when reports critical of the government of India began to draw lessons from the success of Asia's globalization—but the economy was locked into the institutions of import substitution. Economists and political scientists such as Jagdish Bhagwati, T.N. Srinivasan, Padma Desai, Pranab Bardhan, I.G. Patel, and Stanley Kochanek have analysed and described how controls such as industrial and import licenses became a corruption racket. Successful industrialists in import substituting India learned the fine art of procuring licenses by keeping the government of the day in good cheer. They expended resources in rent-seeking activities rather than in improving the quality of their products. If licenses and tariffs could secure monopoly privileges of an elite class of industrialists—they would have an interest in preserving the status quo. Bardhan's *Political Economy of Development in India* (1998) also tells us that the emergence of rich farmers with an interest in garnering ever increasing subsidies, and the class of professionals in the government with an interest in the regime of controls and access to cheap education in the government sector would not easily form a constituency favouring India's globalization.

The foundation of import substitution ideas and the interests they spawned, reveal a great deal about the longevity of import substitution in India. Even though the previous chapter builds on the view that the foundational ideas were being seriously challenged in the 1970s and the 1980s, the ideas and institutions of import substitution were largely intact till 1990. There was gradual deregulation of investment decisions in the 1980s but there was halting globalization during this period. India's trade as a proportion of national income increased only marginally in the 1980s.

Table 2.1 highlights the two salient factors that made an impact on India's global economic engagement. The first is economic ideas. If the government, especially large parts of the technocracy was not convinced about the merit of global economic engagement, there

TABLE 2.1 The Causes of India's Globalization

	Economic Ideas		
	Autarky	Critiquing Autarky	Globalization
Strategic Setting	Non-trader friends	1. 1967–75 Anti-globalization	2. 1975–90 Halting Globalization	3. No episode
	Traders & non-traders as friends	4. 1947–67: Limited globalization	5. No episode	6. 1991– Globalization

would be little possibility for India's integration with the global economy.

A second important factor that impacted India's global economic engagement was the disposition of its friendly countries with respect to global economic integration. Political scientists and economists have drawn attention to the fact that small countries are likely to feel more vulnerable with respect to large countries even though economic integration can produce positive benefits through specialization. This is likely to occur because a smaller country will feel the impact of trade withdrawal at the time of war or economic sanctions to a greater extent than large countries. For example, Bangladesh may gain from a free trade agreement with India but worries that it will feel the pain to a greater extent if India suddenly withdrew from the Bangladesh economy that was deeply integrated with India's. Why then did South Korea, Taiwan, and Singapore not feel similarly vulnerable with respect to the US economy during the Cold War?

Political scientists have pointed out that trade between allies or a friendly country is more likely than commerce between adversaries. What matters is not size but the nature of security relationship. Trade is more likely among allies within a security community where one hegemonic power has a greater stake in the security relationship than smaller countries. The dominant power then has the interest and resources to invest in producing institutions that govern trade among friendly countries. This could be the reason why the US invested in the institutions of trade and economic governance that generated prosperity within the Western alliance. Dean Acheson is known to have famously remarked:

> The preservation and development of sound trading relationships with other countries of the world is an essential and important element in the task of trying build unity and strength in the free world. (Mansfield and Bronson 1991: 104–5)

Trade between the US and the Eastern bloc was negligible by the early 1950s. The US, on the other hand, had stake in the prosperity of Western Europe and South Korea because this prosperity would be an instrument for fighting the Cold War.

This chapter will describe the interaction between economic ideas about globalization and the nature of India's strategic relationships that shaped the content of

India's globalization. Situation 4 in Table 2.1 describes the period between 1947 and 1967. It offered limited possibilities for globalization. The government was a votary of import substitution but was fairly non-aligned during this period. This meant that India maintained almost an equal distance between the US and the USSR during this period. India had cordial relations with traders and non-traders alike. Foreign companies found it relatively easier to operate in India during this period than was the case after 1968, and especially after 1973. This was a time when India's non-alignment and import substitution eventually earned the sympathy of both the US and the USSR. The cut-off date of 1967 is based on the view that 1967 marks the end of a real Indian commitment to non-alignment and a movement towards befriending the USSR. The US approach to India during the balance of payments crisis of 1966 when it coerced India to change its policies to favour trade and the private companies was one reason for the tilt. The second reason lay in the compulsions of India's domestic politics.

Situation 1 describes a situation where India tilted towards the USSR, despite the official proclamation of non-alignment after 1967. This was the anti-globalization phase that lasted from 1967 till 1975. The US's effort to coerce India to devalue the Indian Rupee had hurt the government's pride. India subsequently signed a treaty of friendship and cooperation with Soviet Union in 1971. This was the severest blow to India's credentials as a non-aligned country. India's friends were therefore not the trading countries which were part of the western alliance. The idea of import substitution reached was at its pinnacle between 1968 and 1974, largely due to the compulsions of domestic politics.

Situation 2 describes halting globalization between 1975 and 1990. We believe that the halting liberalization between 1975 and 1990 found the government critiquing import substitution but the institutions of import substitution were largely intact. The political economy of India dominated by industrialists, farmers, and professionals in the bureaucracy obstructed institutional change. Second, India was too friendly with USSR for the US's comfort. India could not officially criticize the Soviet invasion of Afghanistan. Moreover, domestic policies remained autarkic though problems associated with these policies became clear to policymakers during this period. The world of traders would therefore not trust India with a comprehensive trading relationship when India was on the other side of the Cold War and its policies were still largely locked in an import substituting equilibrium.

Situation 6 describes the period of India's globalization. The previous chapter has elaborated on the tipping point model that explains why India embraced globalization and deregulation in 1991 at the time of a Balance of Payment (BoP) crisis. Even though the crisis aided policymakers to deal with powerful vested interests ranged against economic reforms, the critical factor was the ideational milieu within the technocracy. In 1991, a significant number of government economists agreed on and knew that the government needed to globalize and deregulate the economy. In 1966, when the policymakers opined otherwise, import substitution was only reinforced after 1967. 1991 was at a tipping point where the weight of economic ideas supporting globalization and deregulation within the technocracy were further aided by the end of Cold War. The US and its allies would never trust India during the Cold War. India's improved relations with the US and its allies in Asia have had a profound impact on its trade after 1991. India has negotiated free trade agreements with Sri Lanka, Singapore, South Korea, the Association of Southeast Asian Nations and Japan. Indo–US trade, especially service trade is very important, and China is India's largest trading partner. Indo-Sino trade surged from almost nothing in 1991 to $73 billion in 2011–12. This would have been impossible during the Cold War.

We do not find any empirical evidence for Situations 3 and 5. Situation 3 describes a possibility where the Indian government would have embraced globalization as an ideology but found itself in a situation where its friends were not pro-globalization. We do not find evidence that such a hypothetical situation existed in post-colonial India. Similarly, Situation 5 describes a possibility where the government had begun critiquing autarkic industrialization and its foreign relations were good with traders and non-traders alike. Such a scenario did not come to pass in India's post-independence economic history.

This chapter will elaborate on these phases of India's globalization. It will conclude with an analysis of its drivers based on a survey of the economic history of globalization in India.

Limited Globalization: 1947–67

India pursued a strategy of limited globalization in the immediate aftermath of freedom from colonial rule till 1967. This strategy was a product both of a policy of non-alignment and the economic ideology of import substitution industrialization. The policy of import substitution described above stressed on domestic production over imports and exports. And, there was significant commitment to the policy of non-alignment that stressed the imperative to maintain a distance from the politics of the Cold War. India would engage with the US and the Soviet Union but not become a camp follower of either power block.

Non-alignment remained the corner-stone of India's foreign policy during this period. A significant move in the non-alignment movement was Prime Minister Nehru's initiatives to chalk out a block of decolonized countries that would not participate in the Cold War. In the 1940s and the 1950s he tried to forge Sino-Indian solidarity and convince the smaller countries in Asia that they should not feel any threat from either India or China. Since there was to be no threat from the neighborhood, there was no need for Asian countries to ally with the super powers. He tried to stress that India could live peacefully with China following the five 'pancasila' principles of peaceful coexistence. An Asian Relations Conference was held in New Delhi in 1947 to display solidarity among the decolonized nations. India only agreed to a low-key participation in the Baguio conference in Indonesia because Nehru feared that conference involving Carlos Romulo of Philippines, Chiang Kai-Shek of China, and Syngman Rhee of South Korea could become an anti-communist conference. India was concerned that the Colombo Powers Conference in 1954 raised the issue of a communist threat.

The US and the Soviet Union both worried about India's independent foreign policy during the early years. US Secretary of State John Foster Dulles omitted India from his Asia trip in 1953. The US also opposed India's participation in the Far Eastern Political Conference the same year. The Soviet Premier Joseph Stalin refused to meet Nehru's sister and India's first ambassador—Vijaya Laxmi Pandit. The Soviet position began to change only after 1952. The Soviet position on Kashmir became more favourable towards India's and Stalin personally met the second Indian Ambassador Krishna Menon.

The subsequent Bandung Conference held in Indonesia in April 1955 was to highlight the solidarity of the decolonized world through a non-aligned engagement with the super powers. Peaceful and cooperative Sino-Indian relations that comforted the rest of Asia were to be the fulcrum of non-alignment in Asia. Nehru succeeded in temporarily discouraging Laos and Cambodia from entering the Cold War by participating in the Southeast Asia Treaty Organization. Prince Norodum Sihanouk of Cambodia visited Delhi in March 1955 just weeks before the conference. This visit was followed by another visit by Foreign Minister Pham Van Dong of Vietnam in April 1955. Prime Minister Nehru succeeded in convincing the Chinese Premier Zhou Enlai, Burmese Premier U. Nu, Pham Van Dong, and Norodum Sihanouk to pledge allegiance to the 'pancasila principles'.

The Indian government's economic ideology earned the ire of the US in the early years. While non-alignment remained the cornerstone of India's foreign policy in the 1950s, India's developmental ideology favoured import substitution rather than globalization. The United States had eyed a special economic relationship with India since pre-colonial times which had been denied by the British. Soon after independence from British rule in 1947, the US presented a 'Draft Treaty of Friendship, Commerce, and Navigation' in 1948. The treaty sought to promote trade and foreign investment between India and the US but was met with a negative response from India. The Industrial Policy Resolution of 1948 followed by the Industrial Development and Regulation Act (1956) increasingly brought large parts of the industrial sector within the direction of the state. Moreover, the Second Five-Year Plan (1956–61) emphasized state direction and import substitution rather than trade promotion.

Non-alignment and import substitution drove India to adopt a strategy of limited globalization. India would not aggressively pursue trade or foreign investment but would seek assistance both from the US and the USSR. It became clear to policymakers that import substitution was rather import-dependent. India needed both foreign finance and cheap sources of food supply during this period. The strategy of limited globalization involved exploiting super power rivalry to fund India's development. This strategy of globalization was most successful between 1955 and 1962.

The Second Five-Year Plan (1956–61) was a capital-intensive planning model that would demand large doses of foreign assistance. The most significant donor between 1950 and 1955 was the US, which had provided about US$500 million in aid during that period. India would need greater sums during the Second and Third Five-Year Plans to implement its strategy of import substituting capital intensive development. Indian policymakers exploited the USSR's interest in India. This enhanced the US's urge to support India partly because of the US-Soviet rivalry. Despite its prickly policy of non-alignment, India had steered away from communism and protected the institutions of democracy. These were good reasons for the US government to compete with the Soviets in their support for India.

The Soviet Premier Khrushchev (1953–64) took a keen interest in developments in India. Nehru's famous trip to the USSR in 1955 was reciprocated the same year by Khrushchev and Bulganin. India and the USSR shared similar views on disarmament, Indo-China and the United Nation's (UN) rights over

Taiwan. It appreciated India's anti-colonial struggle. India's Second Five-Year Plan had been inspired by a Soviet planning model of 1928 and capital-intensive import substitution appealed to the Soviets. At the Avadi Session of the Indian National Congress early in 1955, a resolution was adopted to promote a socialist pattern of society. Soviet support for India's planned socialist development generated funds for a steel plant in Bhillai on favourable terms when the West was not keen on supporting capital-intensive Indian public sector projects. Even though aid from countries of the Eastern bloc was only 8 per cent of total aid between 1951 and 1968, Khrushchev asserted that Soviet aid was a form of Western aid because it inspired Western countries to be more generous with aid to India. Trade with the Eastern bloc at this time was about 20 per cent of India's trade.

The US also became interested in supporting Indian planning around this time, driven by competition from the USSR and India's credentials as a liberal democracy. In January 1957 the National Security Council opined that the risks from a vulnerable India were greater than one from a strong India because a vulnerable India would increase anti-communist appeal world-wide. There was also considerable support for import substituting industrialization among American development economists in the 1950s. American financing efforts fructified through the US's Development Loan Fund, the World Bank's International Development Association, and the creation of the Aid India Consortium. Between 1951 and 1966 about 51 per cent of India's external assistance came from the US when the same figure was 11 per cent for Soviet Union and the Eastern bloc.

The growing Indo-US interaction revealed the evolving depth of the relationship after 1955. Prime Minister Nehru spent over half a day in President Eisenhower's private farm in Gettysburg in 1956. Influential economists such as Walt Rostow and Max Millikan of the Massachusetts Institute of Technology (MIT) supported rapid heavy industrialization as a strategy called 'big push' which resembled India's import substitution. One of India's senior representatives in Washington, I.G. Patel, noted that these economists along with P.N. Rodenstein Rodan did a signal service by providing intellectual support for India's planning programme. Support was especially critical when India's Second Five-Year Plan ran into financial difficulties in 1957.

There was bi-partisan support for India within the US senate. Democratic Senator John F. Kennedy and Republican Senator Sherman Cooper urged the senate to actively participate in India's development. Under Secretary of State Douglas Dillon and Secretary of State Christian Herter worked closely with the World Bank President Eugene Black to craft the Aid India Consortium. Kennedy's assent to presidency (1961) and his appointment of Harvard economist John Kenneth Galbraith (1961) as US ambassador to India won the respect of Prime Minister Nehru. The aid figure to India thus grew from US$ 400 million in 1957 to US$ 822 million in 1960. Kennedy became interested in funding India's Third Five-Year Plan (1961–6) to the tune of $1 billion a year of which $500 million was earmarked for providing food assistance under the Public Law (PL) 480 program.

The American PL480 program was a substantial benefit for Indian planners. The Second Five-Year Plan which had invested heavily in industrialization, had reduced the government's investment in agriculture as a proportion of total investment. It was opined that organizational changes such as land reforms and rural cooperatives would compensate for the lack of agricultural investment in India. These aspirations failed to materialize and India's agricultural productivity could not keep pace with the level of hunger. The American government's support price for wheat production had led to bumper wheat stocks worth $6 billion in 1958. Food aid through the PL 480 program could be used as a lever to support the friends of the US. US Ambassador Sherman Cooper had negotiated a food agreement with India in 1956 which was renewed by President Eisenhower in 1960.

India's strategy of non-alignment and import substitution paid rich dividends till 1962. Thereafter the US and the World Bank became sceptical about Indian planning and wished to influence Indian policy in a private sector and trade friendly direction. The Aid India Consortium criticized the lack of Indian private sector participation in the economy. A proposal of US aid worth $900 million for a steel plant in Bokaro failed to materialize, despite Ambassador Galbriath's best efforts in 1963. The USSR responded by supporting the plant in Bokaro in 1964.

American aid-weariness reached its peak during India's BoP crisis in 1966, driven by the failure of Indian monsoons in 1965 and 1966. The real problem was the

shortage of food which could only be addressed by
the PL480 program at that time. India could not afford
food at market prices because it needed to save foreign
exchange for capital-intensive industrialization during the Fourth Five-Year Plan. Defense expenditure
had also increased after wars with China (1962) and
Pakistan (1965). American President Lyndon Johnson
and World Bank President George Woods decided to
use food as a lever to change Indian policy at that time.
This was the first time that the World Bank would
coerce a government to change the trajectory of a
country's economic policies.

The key conditions imposed on India were:

(1)   Rupee devaluation;
(2)   freer imports of intermediate goods;
(3)   population control; and
(4)   increased investment in agriculture

Prime Minister Indira Gandhi was quite inexperi-
enced in 1966 and depended heavily on her advisors
who neither favoured devaluation nor import liberalization—which could well have been part of an Indian
strategy of export-led growth. The majority of Indian
economists and technocrats viewed the global trading

system as being exploitative. Moreover, both the Indian Parliament and the majority of Indian business were opposed to this plan. India devalued the Rupee under pressure briefly in 1966. When the BoP situation improved in 1966, it took the decision to veer more towards autarkic state-directed industrialization than in the past. The one area where India and the US agreed was greater investment in technology and resources in Indian agriculture. This became the basis of Indo-US cooperation that produced the green revolution in India.

Apart from the coercive element in aid, India was unhappy for two other significant reasons. First, the US non-project aid figure was substantially less than the $900 million that was promised in 1966. Second, Prime Minister Indira Gandhi was politically inse-cure at this time. Scholars have opined that Nehru's daughter was appointed as a stop gap prime minister by senior contenders for power who belonged to a group called the 'syndicate' within the Congress Party. Indira Gandhi's support base, on the other hand, was with the left within the Congress Party and the Communist Party of India (CPI). She could therefore not become a votary of globalization when the domestic constituencies that would secure her power did not favour it. The strategy of limited globalization would soon be overtaken by a period of anti-globalization approach to development.

Anti-Globalization: 1967–75

India remained nominally non-aligned during this period but the tilt towards the Soviet Union became quite pronounced during this period. Prime Minister Indira Gandhi became dependent on the left within the Congress Party and the CPI to consolidate her power. Moreover dealing with the US during the presidency of Lyndon Johnson hurt India's pride. It was forced to devalue the rupee when the government did not repose faith in that policy. And this devaluation, the government opined, was not appropriately rewarded with aid. The government reacted by capturing the commanding heights of the Indian economy in a manner that was not evident even under Nehru's stewardship of the Indian government. And, the Indian state would move discretely closer to the USSR in the geopolitical world. The combination of friends who were not traders and an economic ideology of import substitution resulted in a phase of anti–globalization at a time when the large parts of Asia would use trade as part of their strategy of development. India's trade as a proportion of national income which was 10 per cent in 1961, dipped to 8 per cent in 1971.

State direction became pronounced in a number of ways that discouraged private and foreign investment in a manner that was unthinkable in the past. A number of government reports since the mid-1960s highlighted the problem of monopolistic Indian private companies that were concentrating wealth among a few stakeholders. Such ideas inspired legislation of the Monopolies and Restrictive Trade Practices (MRTP) Act in 1969, which stringently regulated all Indian companies and interconnected undertakings with gross assets greater than Rupees 200 million. The Industrial Licensing Policy (8 February 1970) made it more difficult for private companies to obtain production licenses. Ideas critical about the participation of foreign companies in the Indian economy emerged from the report of the Mudaliar Committee in 1966. The committee had recommended a Foreign Investment Board that had taken a negative view of foreign investment as development finance. The subsequent

Foreign Exchange Regulation Act (1973) discouraged any investment exceeding Rs 20 million or where the foreign equity share was greater than 40 per cent. The most stringent import control regime was in place between 1970 and 1976. Banks, insurance, and wheat production were all nationalized during this period.

India came closest to being aligned with the USSR during this period. It signed a treaty of peace and cooperation with the USSR in 1971, which provided significant security guarantees. It was on the strength of this treaty that India scored a decisive military victory in a war with Pakistan in 1971. The treaty ensured that China would not open a new front. And, the nuclear powered USS Enterprise, which was hovering around the Arabian Sea, could do no harm. The fact that India's close ties with USSR helped it score a decisive victory against a US ally did not go well with the Americans.

Given the government's intense disposition towards state-led import substitution and its close ties with the USSR, the US was no longer convinced about an economic relationship with India. US external assistance, which was 51 per cent of total external assistance between 1951 and 1966 dipped to 1 per cent in 1975. The World Bank, however, continued to engage with

India. While it is well known that the USSR became deeply involved with the Indian economy, it is hard to obtain the actual aid figure. The transition from limited globalization to a strategy of anti-globalization was one where India's import substitution had to change gears from benefiting from both the Cold warriors to extracting benefits from the one super power that did not believe in trade and financial integration.

Halting Globalization: 1975–90

This was period when India tried hard to woo the US. But its close ties with the USSR stood in the way of security and economic cooperation with US allies. The ties with the USSR remained very deep. As long as the USSR remained, the US would not trust India in a security relationship. The Indian economy began to open up very gradually during this period. India's trade as a proportion of its GDP grew rather gradually from 14 to 18 per cent between 1980 and 1990, and foreign investment was negligible during this period. Even though policymakers became critical of previous policy and wished to shift gears from import substitution to deregulation and globalization, India's political economy was locked in an import substituting equilibrium. This saga of gradual ideational and policy changes favouring deregulation and globalization is detailed in the previous chapter.

India's foreign policy was intimately tied to the USSR. When the Congress Party lost elections having governed India from 1947 till 1977, the US expected the Indian government to change its attitude towards the US. President Carter even visited India soon after the Janata Party was voted to power in 1977. The Janata Party, however, soon realized that the Indo-Soviet Treaty of Friendship and Cooperation would remain the fulcrum of India's security policy. In April 1977, Soviet Foreign Minister Andrei Gromyko offered India Rs 2.25 billion credit on very lenient terms. This was non-project aid that the Government of India could use just as it desired.

The American critics of an aid relationship with India did not favour renewal of aid for a variety of reasons. First, US food aid to India in the 1960s had led to the Indian government's neglect of Indian agriculture. Second, economic assistance had been used to finance government rather than private companies. Third, this aid was used to protect inefficient public and private sector companies in India. Finally, India did not easily accept performance requirements and funding conditions. The friends of India, on the other hand, opined that US had lost a real opportunity in the 1960s. They opined, had President Lyndon Johnson been less coercive, US would have been able to engage India in the 1970s. This debate could not provide the basis for a cooperative Indo-US relationship.

The Cold War forced India to take a decisive stand on Indo-Soviet relations. India sided with Soviet Union when it invaded Afghanistan in December 1979, despite its moral opposition to the intervention. India was deeply disturbed, but favoured the Soviet Union at the United Nations. When the Soviets entered Afghanistan, Pakistan became the frontline state that would serve US interests in the region. This prompted the US to provide a generous $3.2 billion aid package to Pakistan.

This Cold War context did not augur well for harmonious Indo-US economic relations. The US abstained from voting for India's request of $5 billion from the International Monetary Fund (IMF) in the aftermath of the second oil shock in 1980. India secured this loan despite American unease regarding it. The US systematically declined India's request on high technology cooperation because it worried about the leakage of this technology to Soviet Union. It was difficult to obtain fuel for the nuclear power plant in Tarapur. When India requested the power Cray XMP 24 supercomputer, it received only a substantially less technologically-sophisticated Cray XMP 14.

India's trade and investment relationship with the US was marred with problems during this period. The US threatened to restrict India's exports under the Omnibus Trade and Competitiveness Act of 1988. American pharmaceutical companies desired greater protection of property rights. In 1990, US foreign investment in India was a miniscule $19 million.

Not only did the Cold War affect India's relations with the US, it had a negative impact on its relations with the friends of the US in South and Southeast Asia. Indian diplomacy hesitated to relate itself with US allies in Southeast and East Asia. These countries feared Soviet Union and its friends in the region. India was indifferent to Malaysia's invitations to dialogue with the Association of Southeast Asian Nations (ASEAN) in 1975 and in 1980. India supported Soviet backed Heng Samrin when he became chairman of the People's Revolutionary Council of Kampuchea in 1979—an act that drew ire of all the American allies in the ASEAN. The Soviet invasion of Afghanistan was not viewed in a positive light. Visits by Prime Minister Indira Gandhi and Foreign Minister P.V. Narasimha Rao in 1981 failed to yield results. Nor could Prime Minister Rajiv Gandhi (1984–9) make any headway with ASEAN countries. US allies had initially viewed his premiership with optimism but backed out when they found India to be too close to the Soviet-backed regime in Vietnam.

India endured halting globalization from 1975 to 1990 for two substantial reasons. Such globalization was aided by increasing consensus within the government that globalization and deregulation was the way for India's future. The government's economic policy measures favouring deregulation and globalization have been described in the previous chapter. There was minor de-licensing of sectors such as pharmaceuticals, information technology, and auto-parts. The stipulations of the MRTP Act (1969) were diluted to some extent. There was some relaxation in import controls that could feed India's emerging competitiveness in sectors such as information technology.

But India's halting globalization in the 1980s paled in significance with rest of Asia and India's own transformation of economic trajectory in 1991—for two significant reasons. First, the political economy of import substitution was quite entrenched. Powerful industrialists and farmers did not find gains from globalization. An Indian industrial class that had perfected the art of protecting monopolies by securing import and production licenses by maintaining excellent relations with government, had no reason to take on more domestic and global competition that would inevitably accompany a strategy of globalization and deregulation. Second, India was still on the side of the Soviet Union during the Cold War, whose friends were not known to be traders. Cooperation in trade, especially in high technology would therefore be difficult to sustain in a trading world which shared excellent relations with the US's arch enemy the Soviet Union.

Globalization: 1991 Onwards

The fall of the Berlin Wall, substantial changes in the government's view favouring globalization, and the BoP crisis of 1991—all contributed to India's embrace with globalization. The critical factor however, was the change in the government's view about globalization, aided by its own evaluation of policy failures in relation to the rise of Asia. In 1966, India could have turned limited globalization into a full-fledged strategy of globalization, if it had concurred with the US and the World Bank on financing conditions. But India devalued the Rupee under pressure in 1966 and opted for the most stringent version of import substitution soon thereafter. Such a response meant that policy consensus in Delhi was at a great distance from the one in Washington.

We discuss in the previous chapter the substantial role played by Prime Minister P.V. Narasimha Rao and his policy team headed by Finance Minister Manmohan Singh in the summer of 1991. This time, unlike in 1966, the government was convinced of the need for globalization and deregulation, and successfully exploited India's dependence on the IMF at the time of a financial crisis precipitated by the Gulf War. The shock to India's foreign exchange reserves owing to a rise in the price of oil in 1991 was not greater than the two previous shocks in 1973 and 1979. But this time, when the government was spending beyond its means, even this minor shock had far-reaching consequences for financing India's essential imports when foreign commercial banks and non-resident Indians withdrew their financial support for the Indian economy.

The crisis enabled the Indian executive to make virtue of necessity by exploiting the dependence of India's import substituting industry on the IMF. Indian industry needed imports of raw materials and intermediate goods such as machinery for domestic production and oil. Since IMF was the lender of the last resort at a time when India's foreign exchange reserves had hit rock bottom—the government could use this as a lever to gain the acquiescence of Indian industry to conditions without which IMF funding would not be available. I have argued elsewhere that the government had a home-grown programme that was tested in the 1980s which was also aligned more closely with the Washington consensus in 1991 than was the case in 1966. It was this home-grown New Delhi consensus that enabled the government to seize this opportunity to deregulate and globalize the economy. The currency was devalued; import restrictions were drastically curbed; and foreign direct investment would now be more welcome than ever before. India's stock markets were disciplined to attract portfolio investment from abroad to strengthen Indian companies. Mutual funds abroad invested in India through the portfolio route, impressed by the growth potential of a major emerging economy. These constituted the main planks of India's strategy of globalization.

The fall of the Berlin Wall in 1990 was an additional benefit for policymakers to pursue India's strategy of globalization. The Soviet Union had retreated from Afghanistan in 1988. Moreover, the country itself had disintegrated into smaller units. When the US's arch enemy had collapsed, it became possible for the Indian government to relate with the US, its trading allies, and multilateral institutions in a manner that was impossible in the past.

Russia's strategic and commercial value to India also declined considerably after the Cold War's end. Imports of defence equipment suffered procurement delays after the Soviet Union disintegrated into a number of countries. Also, the trade between India and the Soviet Union which had been based on preferential treatment and barter ceased. If India could procure defence equipment in return for wheat, it now needed to pay in hard currency. When the rouble depreciated after the Cold War the exchange rate at which India's trade would be settled became a matter of serious dispute. Such were the nature of these differences that India decided to curb its exports to the USSR in 1991. India's imports of crude oil from the USSR declined the same year. India's export share to Russia and the former Soviet Union dipped from 20.4 per cent of its exports in 1985 to 3.6 per cent in 1995.

Shifts in ideas favouring economic globalization at the end of the Cold War necessitated institutional changes. India's Ministry of External Affairs needed to increase its foreign economic engagement. More importantly the Ministry of Commerce and Industry (MOCI) enhanced its diplomatic engagement. The Trade Policy Division within MOCI became an important department. Inter-ministerial coordination on issues such as intellectual property and agricultural price supports was also upgraded. These issues required dialogue between ministries and policy think tanks that understood domestic requirements with those that could engage fruitfully with the rest of the world.

The global shift in India's trade has been quite dramatic. India's merchandize exports to Russia and the former Soviet Union declined from over $15 billion in 1990 to about a billion dollars in 2005. Even though merchandise exports to the US increased only marginally from $15 billion in 1990, the US became the most voracious consumer of its information technology (IT) and IT-enabled service exports. More than 60 per cent of these exports that have secured for India the status of the world's 'back office' went to the US. Such has been the impact of these exports that authors such as Thomas Friedman have argued that information technology has made the world flat as Indians are not only producing software but are also tutoring, accounting, and provide state of the art research and development services over the internet. This business is likely to earn India about $70 billion in the current year.

The Indian diaspora has emerged as one of the most highly educated, wealthy, and powerful in the US. They have exploited the post–Cold War world and domestic conditions in India to promote the cause of Indo-US relations. Silicon Valley networks have helped the software industry in India to globalize. Most recently, the Indian diaspora in the US played a critical role in helping the US government overcome bottlenecks to a nuclear deal with India which not only freed trade in nuclear fuels but also opened the way for Indo-US trade in sensitive technologies that the US would never have shared during the Cold War. The diaspora-funded lobbyists helped create the India Caucus in the Congress and the Friends of India Caucus in the Senate. The Indian American Forum for Political Education and the spirited leadership of Swadesh Chatterjee played a silent but important role in drawing the Indian and American business communities together and lobbying for India within the Congress and the Senate.

There were limitations to Sino-Indian relations during the Cold War when China grew rapidly after befriending the US and distancing itself from the Soviet Union in the 1970s. That too changed quite dramatically in the post-Cold War world, despite the legacy of the Sino-Indian war in 1962 and unsettled borders. When China and India had both decided to use economic globalization as a path to development, much like the rest of Asia—they could separate their security relationship from their trade relationship. Trade has expanded rapidly from almost nothing in 1990 to over \$73 billion in 2011–12—making China, India's largest trading partner. This occurred despite a \$27 billion trade deficit for India.

The Sino-Indian economic engagement is quite intensive. Chinese companies are manufacturing 30 to 35 per cent of the power plants in India and its telecom companies command about 35 per cent of the wireless market. Lenovo leads the Indian personal computer market. India's presence in the Chinese market though less is quite significant. Mahindra's have garnered 9 per cent of the tractor market—second only to John Deere. Binani Cements has a sizable operation. The National Institute of Information Technology (NIIT) has 205 centres in China. The Tata group of industries is present across the spectrum and its two automobile brands Landrover and Jaguar have opened joint ventures with Chery. Other major Indian companies operating in China include: Infosys, WIPRO, Bharat Forge, Thermax, Sundram Fasteners, Dr. Reddy's, and Birlas.

Trade with Southeast Asia has picked up too. We found that Southeast Asia was unwilling to have a dialogue with India during the Cold War. Now that the Cold War had ended and India wanted to globalize, substantial possibilities for cooperation have arisen. India was offered the status of a sectoral dialogue partner of the ASEAN in 1992 and promoted to a full-fledged dialogue partner in 1995. In 1996, India was invited to the ASEAN Regional Forum which is a conference on security dialogue in the Southeast Asian region. In December 2005, India was also invited to the East Asia Summit comprising of ASEAN, China, Japan, Australia, and New Zealand.

Singapore has been one of the pillars of India's look east policy. Finance Minister Manmohan Singh had visited Malaysia and Singapore in April 1991 during the BoP crisis. This was the finance minister's first trip abroad. Subsequently Prime Minister Rao undertook a trip to Japan in 1992. In his historic Singapore lecture delivered at the Institute of Southeast Asian Studies in 1994, Rao defined the role of the non-resident Indian in fostering the development of the motherland.

The Comprehensive Economic Cooperation Agreement with Singapore in 2005 is a landmark agreement. It was the first comprehensive free trade agreement signed by India. The agreement was a way to thank Singapore for helping India find a place in Asia, which had eluded it during the Cold War. It was easy for a free trader like Singapore to make asymmetrical concessions. Singapore is one of the most open economies in the world with a trade to GDP ratio of about 400 per cent. The agreement was supposed to facilitate Singapore's investment in India in addition to promoting trade. Both these aspirations have been realized. Trade between India and Singapore at $25.4 billion was greater than India's trade with all of South Asia ($15.8 billion) in 2011–12. It took India much longer to negotiate a free trade agreement (FTA) with ASEAN (2010) because of substantial differences over the large Indian negative list of commodities. The Indo-ASEAN FTA will further promote India's trade, especially if ASEAN becomes more forthcoming in accepting India's service exports.

Korea and India have also inked a free trade agreement in 2010. Trade between the two countries is worth $20 billion. Korea was one of the first countries to move into the Indian market. Hyundai cars, and LG and Samsung's electronic equipments are extremely popular in India. Korean brands in India are better known than the country's own. The Pohang Steel Plant has pledged a $12 billion investment in iron ore extraction and iron and steel plants in Orissa. Moreover, the end of the Cold War and India's Look East Policy helped the relationship grow at a time when

Pakistan was participating in covert security cooperation with South Korea's arch enemy—North Korea.
Korea and India are in serious discussions about cooperation in sensitive areas such as nuclear and defence
technology.

India has a trade agreement with Japan as well
(2010). Japan's trade with India at $17.8 billion
(2011–12) is well below potential. India's relations with
Japan have been cemented both by the end of the Cold
War as well as worries about Chinese expansionism.
Even though Japan is not India's largest trader or investor it has invested $4.5 billion in a road network called
the Golden Quadrilateral that will connect Delhi to
Mumbai and has the provision of seven new cities in
the states of Uttar Pradesh, Madhya Pradesh, Haryana,
Gujarat, Rajasthan, and Maharashtra. Japan's overseas
development assistance has been to India substantial.
The country is deeply involved with India's infrastructure development. Given the limitations of geography
and size faced by Japan, and India's excellent location
and rapid economic growth, Japanese companies are
keen to invest in India to gain a foothold in that market.
They would also like to use India as a base to export to
Europe and the middle-east from India.

Paradoxically enough, India's own neighbours are not integrated with the Indian economy even though it constitutes over 80 per cent of the region's GDP. India's trade with South Asia is less than 5 per cent of its trade with the world. Worries about Indian hegemony abound. In addition, the history of Indo-Pakistan relations has not been comforting for the region. Pakistan has tied its economic relationship with India to its territorial claims over the northern frontier state of Kashmir. Since Pakistan is a muslim majority country and considers itself to be an Islamic state, it wishes to exercise a right over India's Kashmir, which has a muslim majority. India, on the other hand, is a secular country where citizenship and faith are supposed to be unrelated. Kashmir therefore cannot easily be separated from India on the basis of religion. India has fought three wars with Pakistan. The last one in 1971 partitioned Pakistan into Pakistan and Bangladesh. These memories of conflict do not augur well for economic cooperation. Despite these problems, important constituencies in Pakistan realize that trade with India is essential for the country as it has the potential of replacing expensive imports with cheaper ones from India, and also for promoting its exports.

India's economic growth has increasingly become appealing for Pakistani policymakers. These changes in Pakistan's perception of India, and the ease of visa restrictions may open the way for the relationship to be driven along the lines of the Sino-Indian relationship. The low trade figure of $1.9 billion (2011–12) is a product of security relations rather than the economic imperatives facing the two countries.

The South Asian Association for Regional Cooperation (SAARC) established in 1985 was largely unsuccessful in promoting economic cooperation, despite the South Asian Preferential Trade Agreement (SAPTA, 1995) and the South Asian Free Trade Agreement (SAFTA, 2005). Nepal, Bhutan, and Maldives enjoy asymmetrical concessions under SAFTA. These concessions did not boost intra-South Asian trade because India has free trade agreements with Nepal and Bhutan and citizens of these countries do not need a visa to travel to either of these countries.

Bilateral trade with Bangladesh at $4.3 billion (2011–12) has grown quite remarkably in recent years. The two countries have had ongoing negotiations about border fairs which have the potential to raise this trade to $25 billion. Illegal trade nevertheless constitutes about 75 per cent the value of legal trade between the countries. India's relations with the country have improved remarkably after the assent of Sheikh Hasina to premiership in 2009. India offered a $1 billion aid package to the country to help consolidate relations between the two countries.

India's trade with Sri Lanka at $5.1 billion (2011–12) benefited from the Indo-Sri Lanka Free Trade Agreement (ISFTA). This was India's first free trade agreement (2000) even though it was less comprehensive than the one with Singapore. Though this trade figure is below potential and the countries have failed to negotiate an agreement on services with India, it must be remembered that Sri Lanka has a population of about 20 million people, whereas both Pakistan and Bangladesh have more than a 150 million. The trade figure is therefore more significant considering Sri Lanka's relatively small population.

A number of factors engendered this agreement. First, the end of Cold War was helpful because Sri Lanka's relations with the US had been excellent. In the early 1990s Indian and Sri Lankan economists conducted a study on the possibilities of trade and economic integration pointing out the opportunities lost for Indo-Sri Lanka trade relations as a result of intra-South Asian protectionism. It must be remembered that Sri Lanka adopted a strategy of economic globalization in 1977. It was the first South Asian country to embark on that path. Second, the militant Liberation Tigers of Tamil Eelam (LTTE) had stood in the way of cordial relations between the two countries. India had worried that the Sinhala majority was discriminating against the large Tamil population in the northeast of Sri Lanka. This issue was quickly sorted out when an LTTE terrorist assassinated former Prime Minister Rajiv Gandhi on the eve of the India's elections in May 1991. India withdrew its support for the LTTE. 1991 was also the year when India boldly embarked on its strategy of economic globalization. Globalization, geopolitics, and South Asian politics rapidly transformed economic relations by the creation of a Joint Commission that dealt with trade, finance, and investment between India and Sri Lanka. As India globalized, liberal doctrines such as the Gujral doctrine—aptly named after the former Prime Minister I.K. Gujral (April 1997 to March 1998)—ensured that India would more than reciprocate any gestures made by a small South Asian neighbour.

The Indo-Sri Lanka FTA was further aided by two external events—the Asian financial crisis in 1997 and India's nuclear tests in 1998. First, the Asian financial crisis worried India because Asia had been an inspiration for India's globalization, but the same region was facing an economic recession after 1997. The critics of India's globalization therefore argued that India's globalization was a misplaced idea when tiger economies of Asia such as South Korea were reeling under a recession. Second, India's nuclear tests in 1991 provoked sanctions by significant trading countries such as the US and Japan. India desperately needed to locate new markets at a time when it had betted on a strategy of economic globalization.

India's globalization, the end of Cold War, and external shocks—all inspired India to make asymmetrical concessions towards a smaller neighbour. This addressed the worries of protectionist lobbies in Sri Lanka. India provided concessions for 1,000 items whereas Sri Lanka provided the same for 300. India would reduce its tariffs to zero in three years but Sri Lanka was given eight years to execute the adjustment. India placed about 75 per cent of its goods on the free trade list whereas the same figure for Sri Lanka was 49 per cent. These measures provided a philip for Indo-Sri Lanka trade. Between 1999 and 2005, Sri Lanka's exports to India grew from 1 per cent to 9 per cent. The same figures for imports were 8.5 per cent and 20.7 per cent, respectively.

Trade and globalization have produced economic growth which has transformed India from a major recipient of foreign aid to a significant donor. India was the largest recipient of foreign aid between 1951 and 1992—receiving $55 billion in aid. In 2011, on the other hand, India disbursed $1.5 billion in foreign aid—second only to China among developing countries. The country is creating a national aid agency. India's foreign aid is geared towards pursuing the country's strategic interests. A few examples will highlight the relationship between India's aid and its commercial interest. Assistance has been provided to Iran to build a port at Chabahar. India happens to be the second largest importer of Iranian oil. India is constructing roads to the Afghan city of Hajigak—a place where the National Mineral Development Corporation and the Steel Authority of India have won mining rights. India is Afghanistan's fifth largest donor. The country pledged $1 billion to Bangladesh in development aid

(2010), hoping that Shiekh Hasina's friendly government will capitalize on it and build lasting economic
ties with India. India's special envoy is negotiating a
peace agreement in Khartoum at a time when India's
oil imports from Southern Sudan have become quite
significant. India also pledged $5 billion in aid to Africa
at the India–Africa Forum Summit in 2011.

More significantly, the global financial crisis found
India playing a significant role in the Group of 20
(G-20) nations. It became important to expand the
G-7 to include India, China, and other emerging
economies at a time when the West could not man-
age the rest. Whereas India was facing IMF and World
Bank conditions during BoP crises in 1966 and 1991,
the country participates in discussions about how
developed economies in Europe should adjust to the
current crisis. It also pledges loans to bail some of these
developed countries out of a crisis. India's globalization
is transforming the country from being a recipient of
conditionalities to being one of its architects.

Indian companies have achieved a global footprint
that surpasses that of the Indian state. India's outward
foreign investment is more spectacular than inward

investment. Sixty-one per cent of the global sales and 30 per cent of the Tata Group's 3, 50,000 employees resided outside India in 2008. The company purchased the Anglo-Dutch steel maker Corus Steel for $12.1 billion—one of the largest deals in the history of the steel industry. The Tata Group also purchased named auto brands such as Landrover and Jaguar, propelling it into the elite league of auto makers. These foreign subsidiaries would benefit from linkages back home with companies such as Tata Steel and Tata Motors. Similarly, Bharat Forge is one of the world's leading producers of machine components for the pre-eminent auto makers. With operations in China, US, Germany, North America, Sweden, and Scotland, the company is second only to Thyssen Krupp of Germany and ahead of Sumitomo Metal of Japan. These are only two examples of the global footprint of some of India's smartest companies. India is a leading foreign investor in Britain. In 2006, Indian companies invested $12.8 billion abroad. Indian outflows accounted for 6 per cent of the total outflows from developing countries whereas China's outflows were 9 per cent of developing country investments. This was a very high figure considering that the Chinese economy was two and half times the Indian economy.

* * *

This chapter has argued that the trajectory of India's economic globalization was shaped substantially by two important factors—the government's ideology and the nature of its external relations. Non-alignment and import substitution produced a phase of limited globalization between 1947 and 1967 when India successfully exploited the Cold War to pursue import substitution or economic self-sufficiency rather than trade and global economic integration. Cold War rivalry was used rather efficiently for domestic economic purposes.

The subsequent period from 1967 till 1975 was an anti-globalization phase when the ideology of state command and import substitution were at their pinnacle. This was also the period when India was closely aligned to the Soviet Union—a fact that became very evident after the Indo-Soviet Treaty of Friendship and Cooperation in 1971. Anti-globalization ideology coupled with close and almost exclusive ties with Soviet Union and its allies cemented the anti-globalization phase in India's foreign economic relations.

Halting liberalization from 1975 to 1990 was the product of changing government ideology increasingly critiquing the import substitution past which was embedded in a political economy that did not favour globalization. The domestic constraints to globalization were quite significant during this period when powerful Indian industrialists were not willing to engage with greater domestic and international competition. In addition, India remained so closely tied to Soviet security and economic guarantees that it would be difficult for the country to earn the trust of the US.

India's embrace with globalization beyond the Cold War (1991 and beyond) benefited both from the changed ideology of the government and the disappearance of the Soviet Union. If there was no Soviet Union on the political horizon why would the US bother about India's ties with its former arch enemy? Moreover, the BoP crisis of 1991 provided an opportunity for the government to deal with political opponents of globalization to stamp its mark of globalization on the Indian economy. India's economic relations with the US and its allies in Asia improved remarkably as its economic ties with Russia and the former Soviet

Union became less significant. Its economic relations with neighbours in South Asia, though less significant, have also witnessed some improvement. India now has a global profile as a foreign aid provider, as a source of outward foreign investment, and as a significant participant in the G-20.

3

Citizen Concern in the New India

States, especially those that repose faith in democracy are populated with citizens who have a direct relationship with the state through taxation. States tax citizens and in return citizens are entitled to a variety of benefits. What produced this relationship? Charles Tilly, for example, tells us that warfare conducted by the state produced the citizen in Europe. As the costs of war escalated, monarchs needed to raise resources from their subjects to finance wars. But the subjects could not be easily coerced and the monarchs had finally to give back something in return for resources they parted with. This, according to Tilly, was the birth of the citizen in Europe—'[S]tates made wars and wars made the state'. The citizen and the state thus became two sides of the same coin. Other scholars such as Acemoglu and Robinson (2012) have argued that welfare and citizenship arose due to the need of the capitalist class to keep the peace workers. This Chapter describes why citizen concern has been lacking in India and what explains its evolution in recent times. It also reflects on the possible pathways out of this conundrum.

Has democracy empowered the Indian citizen? An average Indian lives till the age of 65 years whereas Sri Lankans and Chinese live almost ten years longer. Literacy is an important empowerment tool for any citizen. Whereas in India, 74 per cent are literate, more the 90 per cent of the Chinese and Sri Lankans can read and write. About 41 per cent Indians live on $1.25 (adjusted for purchasing power parity) or less in a day, whereas in China and Sri Lanka, 15.9 per cent and 7 per cent, respectively, live on incomes this low. While these averages hide substantial variation within India because a state like Kerala in southern India, which is more populous than Sri Lanka, may have a life expectancy rate similar to Sri Lanka's, these average figures are cause for alarm. A person born in India therefore has substantially lesser life expectancy than one in neighbouring Sri Lanka or China.

Despite these glaring depredations faced by Indians, economists would generally agree that economic reforms have made an impact on poverty, even though this impact is much less significant than desired. Why have some parts of India achieved higher levels of human development than others? And, despite these glaring inequities and depredations, what explains the birth of welfare in India? This chapter reviews ideas such as patronage democracy that provide clues about why India remains socially backward despite fairly robust economic growth within a democracy. It then highlights three welfare measures—the right to employment, the right to education, and the right to information, which have strengthened the institutions of citizen formation in India in recent times. Like the story of economic growth, the story of citizen formation is a gradual and almost imperceptible one—but it is on its way.

Some scholars have attributed the success of welfare in India to the nature of the political party at the state level. Cadre-based political parties that represented the poor could redistribute land and credit to the marginalized sections of society. Others have argued that the emergence of a political society to be at the root of welfare in India. Members of political society are different from citizens. They drive the state to provide benefits when the state makes exceptions for the poor which are not guaranteed under the constitution as rights. Political parties pander to concerns of political society to remain in power. Political society therefore survives by making exceptions, but not by guaranteeing citizenship rights. Both are powerful arguments about the provision of public services. In addition to these pathways to welfare, we also need to consider the evolution of the idea of citizenship through a plethora of government policies and practices at the central and state levels, which are reinforced by social movements.

The idea that the citizen should have economic rights may also have been reinforced by rapid economic growth described in Chapter 1. When an economy grows rapidly, 1 per cent of the gross domestic product (GDP) becomes a larger figure than in previous years. But whether these resources should be diverted for citizen well-being would still depend on electoral pressures and the way in which politicians view their constituencies. The idea that the state is responsible for the well-being of its citizens is essential for this realization. Ideational changes favouring citizen concern among the elite can steer the polity away from what Kanchan Chandra described as an overarching 'patronage democracy'.

The chapter points to the path of a possible Indian tipping point model of evolving citizenship and welfare where ideas become powerful because of the inability of previous policies to produce desired results in human well-being. This is especially true when new ideas are reinforced by social initiatives and movements. These evolving political ideas gain salience over time and reach a tipping point when they get institutionalized in a manner that appears discontinuous from the past. To give some examples: the idea of official secrecy was replaced by the legitimate need for the citizen to access government information, ideas supporting the need for child labour were replaced by an abhorrence towards depriving children of primary education, and the policy elite's comfort with unemployment and low wage labour was replaced by the guilt that every poor citizen was being deprived meaningful wage employment. Changes in the ideas or morals that drive institutions and shape behaviour can be called institutional change. Institutional change that appears discontinuous is often really an incremental path dependent process where the momentum of ideas and practices brings the system to a tipping point from where transformatory change can occur.

The chapter equally points to other pathways to citizen well-being in India. It takes a close look at arguments that suggest that backward caste or class based parties produce development. It also takes seriously political society as well as non–governmental social initiatives as a route to development. This chapter reviews the empirical and theoretical literature on development of the poor and suggests that one needs to give serious consideration to the tipping point model described above that has more to do with changes in ideas among the elite as a harbinger of mobilizing social and economic change in India.

Ways of Thinking about Welfare in India

India's patronage democracy has been a substantial stumbling block obstructing citizenship rights. Political mobilization of backward caste groups did not always produce good developmental outcomes. Ethnic caste-

based voting at the macro level has considerable stay-
ing power in India because it is often difficult for a
voter to decide who the best candidate at the state or
the national level is. But it is relatively easy to identify
the caste of a voter by her surname. Public sector jobs
can become an instrument for patronage that enables
elected leaders to reward members of their own caste
group. If government schools are a major source of
public employment, then former chief minister of
Uttar Pradesh, Mulayam Singh Yadav could reward his
Yadav supporters with jobs in those schools. In this
mode of patronage politics, it is more important to
employ Yadavs as teachers than to improve the quality
of teachers in one of the most socially backward, illiterate and poverty stricken Indian states—Uttar Pradesh.

Patronage democracy can challenge developmental
politics. Sudha Pai found that powerful caste groups
in Madhya Pradesh dominated over the most socially
depressed caste groups (dalits) in Madhya Pradesh. The
state's former chief minister Digvijay Singh attempted
to redistribute land to dalits, empower village governments, and initiated a rather successful education
guarantee scheme (1993–2003). He launched a socially
transformative programme of distributing land to dalits

taken from the common village grazing areas without taking away anyone's land. This was a top-down
government sponsored effort that met with substantial
social opposition. A principle reason why Singh and
the Congress Party have not won an election in the
state after 2003 is that the dalits did not gain from
land distribution and the more numerous and politically powerful backward caste groups turned against
the dalits and the Congress Party after this experiment.
Powerful backward caste groups were habituated to
exploiting their village's common property resources
for personal use. These common property resources
had been earmarked for redistribution by the government. The right-wing Bharatiya Janata Party (BJP) in
opposition mobilized the powerful backward caste
groups who were angered by the government's redistributive move.

Dalits therefore did not gain much from chief
minister Singh's initiative. They were often beaten up
and sometimes even the land transferred to them was
not available for their use. Their crops were destroyed.
Such was the oppositional power of backward caste
groups that Singh announced a 27 per cent reservations
quota for them in government jobs to win back their

political support. The power of the backward caste groups thus blocked welfare and citizen well-being that could have benefited the most socially marginalized group in Madhya Pradesh. The oppressive power of the rural elite rings true in the most backward parts of rural India.

If patronage democracy is socially debilitating, Partha Chatterjee (2011) has argued that political society can empower the poor in a democracy. When the state cannot grant citizenship rights to all, it can provide exceptional exemptions from rules in order to gain legitimacy and remain in power. Squatter groups and street vendors routinely violate the law. They live in slums that are not sanctioned within law. They sell their wares on the streets for which there is neither receipt nor mention in the national accounts. Ignoring these and other illegal activities that are a part of the survival strategy of the urban poor is a good way for any political party to garner public support. The Shiv Sena has used urban squatters to promote the idea of Hindu and Maratha hegemony in Mumbai. Maratha hegemony is the Sena's source of political power. Political society is a persuasive explanation for the coexistence of democracy in the absence of citizenship rights and welfare. Such an explanation is not substantially different from patronage democracy, except that the ways of providing welfare in these cases are in the grey area of law. But political society, like patronage democracy is more about populism than welfare—that too owing to the compulsions of electoral politics.

The empirical work of Corbridge, Williams, and Srivastava (2005) reveals why the distinction between patronage democracy and citizenship is important, even though it is sometimes difficult to treat political society as a purely autonomous social space. For example, the Employment Assurance Scheme that they studied in Midnapore district in West Bengal was working well. Midnapore residents were increasingly behaving like citizens rather than members of political society because they were able to secure their rights in Midnapore. When employment becomes a right, any Indian citizen will be able to rightfully demand it. In Vaishali in the state of Bihar, on the other hand, backward caste dominance ensured that the dominant caste group enjoyed citizenship rights. This narrative is consistent with 'patronage democracy'—where a particular caste group in power was able to benefit from social services provided by the government. To give one example: Laloo Yadav—the iconic chief minister of Bihar ensured that Yadavs could now gain access to the once famous Darbhanga Medical College Hospital's operation theatre when in earlier times only upper caste groups had accessed subsidized and medical treatment in such settings. While such possibilities added to Yadav pride in Bihar—the hospital's sanitary and cleanliness standards now were much inferior to the past. Well-to-do members of the upper caste groups would now only be concerned with private health care.

Another route to welfare provision in India was through parties with a pro-poor social base and ideology. Top down approaches to redistribution and welfare have been successful in such cases. The unambiguously pro-poor anti- landlord ideology of the Communist Party of India (Marxist) (CPI[M]) backed by disciplined party cadres in West Bengal was a change agent in the late 1970s and the early 1980s. The party and its cadres successfully distributed substantial land and credit to the poor after the coming to power in 1977—a factor that helped win elections continuously from 1977 till 2011. Atul Kohli has described the spectacular success of the CPM in West Bengal after 1977.

But even this success story of redistribution has run into rough weather. The proportion of West Bengal's population below the official Indian poverty line is just about the national average. The same social dynamism that had propelled land reforms in West Bengal in the late 1970s seemed to be missing towards the fag end of rule in 2011.

Backward caste dominated political parties in southern India have been more developmental than the ones in northern India. The Dravida Munnetra Kazhagam (DMK), for example, has performed remarkably in providing citizen services to the populace of Tamil Nadu. Such is the power of Dravidian parties in Tamil Nadu that the ruling party has alternated between the two parties—the DMK and the All India Anna Dravida Munnetra Kazhagam (AIADMK) since 1967. The Congress Party has never won elections in the state after 1967. These backward caste parties have worked with a broader social coalition and have delivered welfare in a manner that goes beyond our understanding of patronage democracy. Tamil Nadu's public distribution of food-grains is one of the best in the country. Poor Tamilians consumed 97 per cent of their food entitlement whereas the same figure for Bihar was 45 per cent in 2011. Its mid-day meal scheme has encouraged poor children to go to school. The success of this state-level scheme has turned it into a national project and the world's largest welfare programme of its kind through a decision of the Supreme Court.

More research is required to assess whether the DMK and the AIADMK were driven largely by the ideology of social justice propounded by the intellectual architect of the Dravidian movement—E.V. Ramaswami. Did the caste composition of Tamil Nadu create a ground for this inclusive ideology to work? Narayan Lakshman has argued that the absence of dominant caste groups in Tamil Nadu like Vokkaligas and Lingayats of Karnataka facilitated citizen welfare in the state. Tamil Nadu did not possess a numerically dominant and politically powerful backward caste group which could hold its sway by providing patronage within its kin group. So the backward caste coalition needed to be a broader one. This could be the reason why Tamil Nadu's welfare policies are more broad-based than those in Uttar Pradesh or Karnataka.

Systematic temporal comparisons point to an improvement in citizen well-being in Tamil Nadu.

Harriss, Jeyaranjan and Nagaraj conducted field-work in a Tamil Nadu village in 2008 studied by Gilbert Slater in 1916. The same village had been revisited again by Guhan and Mencher in 1981. The social transformation of the village is a story of change with continuity. The large Reddy landlord wielded power but his absolute authority had diminished. Access to education had improved considerably both for dalit and upper caste families. Piped water had reached the dalit population and electrification had improved considerably. Sanitation standards were still very poor. The sarpanch was a dalit woman and dependent professions such as blacksmiths and carpenters had nearly vanished. Longitudinal studies by scholars such as Djurfeldt, Athreya, Jaykumar, Rajagopal, and Vidyasagar also corroborate this view about Tamil Nadu.

There is something to be said about the rise of a backward caste party in Tamil Nadu whose consequences for citizen welfare were vastly different from the Samajwadi Party's rise in the UP or the Rashtriya Janata Dal's ascent in Bihar. In poorer states like Bihar, for example, officials involved with public distribution of food were routinely bribed and trucks laden with supposedly subsidized food-grains were directed towards the open market. Dismal infrastructure governed the public distribution of food-grains. Social action by journalists and non-governmental organizations (NGOs) though necessary was insufficient for fighting corruption. The approach of the government in Tamil Nadu, on the other hand, was different. The DMK and the AIADMK understood that Congress dominance in the state could only be reversed if poorer backward caste groups enjoyed ample public services like the supply of food-grains. The DMK had not forgotten that it had ridden to power for the first time in the aftermath of a drought and food shortage in 1967. The government spent considerable resources to distribute food within the state. This was backed by sound governance of public distribution of food, which was in stark contrast to the management of food supplies in Bihar or Uttar Pradesh. The collector in Tamil Nadu or the leading administrator of a district was a senior official charged with the responsibility of inspections. Moreover, there was a bi-annual conference of collectors attended by the chief minister. The chief minister routinely oversaw the governance of public distribution of food, and information technology was widely used to track the movement of food-grains in the state.

Apart from political parties, Hindu nationalist social service organizations linked to the right-wing BJP have also promoted welfare in India. Tariq Thachil found that two organizations supported by the BJP—the Vanvasi Kalyan Ashram (VKA) and Sewa Bharti (SB) actively promoted welfare activities such as primary education and health services for poor families in Chhattisgarh—a state neighbouring Madhya Pradesh in central India. Both the organizations had links to Hindu nationalist organizations connected with the BJP. Since Hindu nationalist ideology did not hold much appeal for the tribal people of Chhattisgarh, social workers attempted to win the hearts of the people by voluntarily delivering public services. Their schools performed better than government schools and these organizations provided simple medical services to the poor.

Social service workers with an influence due to their welfare work would approach citizens and try to subtly influence their political views in favour of the BJP. A political conversation could arise during social interactions and workers would explain various voting options to citizens. Even though electoral gain for the BJP was the objective—this goal served the poorest and most socially oppressed caste groups. This approach is different from one where politicians try to satisfy their electorally significant client caste groups by providing them with benefits and government jobs.

There is also evidence to suggest that people in parts of rural India are now increasingly mobilized towards garnering their rights as citizens. Anirudh Krishna found that the new leaders or 'naya netas' of Rajasthan and Madhya Pradesh were better informed and educated, and owned less land than their traditional patrons. These local leaders of rural India did not necessarily belong to a party. Rather ruling parties competed to win the most efficient leaders over to their side—so that service delivery could be efficiently provided under their guidance. These local level leaders helped secure development projects and made them work on the ground. Therefore in areas with good local leaders, the chances were that the development projects would work well.

Non-political non-governmental organizations have initiated social movements that have sought to make the state more accountable. The work of the Mazdoor Kisan Shakti Sangathan (MKSS; Organization for the Rights of Workers and Peasants) in the state of Rajasthan is well known. This organization has pio-

117

neered the idea of the right to information in India. Aruna Roy, an Indian Administrative Services (IAS) officer who resigned from service to form this organization was convinced that the Official Secrets Act (1923)—a legacy from British colonialism stood in the way of service delivery in India. She would organize public meetings in rural Rajasthan to expose the disparity between the funds allocated for citizen welfare and the fruits of such investment. It was often found that there was a wide gap between what the government had pledged and what was available as welfare. For example, MKSS would scrutinize school records to see if a school existed where it should, whether it had the necessary infrastructure, and whether the commissioned school teacher was around when he was supposed to be. If information on welfare investment could be obtained from the government, local citizens in a public hearing ('jan sunwai') would point to the gap between investments and social outcomes which had been filled by corruption. Public hearings at the grass roots level were therefore an excellent way to expose corruption. The idea that citizens had the right to information thus began to acquire some political salience.

The section on the right to information will discuss at greater length the significance of social activists mobilizing people on the ground to actualize the legitimacy of the right to information. This was the birth of an idea that citizens needed access to vital information that had an impact on their well-being. Peasants were mobilized by the MKSS for the first time in village Kot Kirana in Pali district of Rajasthan. Documents related to development expenditure had been earlier obtained unofficially by MKSS. The poor then verified, corroborated, and analysed the information. Thus began a movement spearheaded by activists which would become a Right to Information (RTI) law in the state of Rajasthan in 2000. We discuss in greater detail how this idea became a right that was enacted by the Indian Parliament in 2005.

Further research on bottom-up processes shaping welfare in India will enlighten us on many issues concerned with citizenship. It is possible that such bottom-up processes are making an impact on development and politics in India. Stepan, Linz, and Yadav (2011) have reported that more Indians believed that their vote mattered in 2004 (68 per cent) than in 1971 (48 per cent). Moreover, poorer voters seem less apathetic about elections than richer ones. Perhaps this could be the reason why welfare seemed to be taking over patronage politics in states like Bihar. The politics of patronage worked along a very different logic. Upper caste groups would co-opt lower caste groups to stay in power. Or, the elite among the backward caste parties in power would favour their own caste groups. And, the state would make exceptions to the poor for strategic political reasons rather than provide citizenship rights to the poor to remain in power. Many would agree that Bihar under Chief Minister Nitish Kumar has turned the corner in its transition away from patronage politics since 2005. The government in Bihar now pays more attention to the overall development of the state rather than prefer a few strategic ethnic communities.

Ideas, Tipping Point, and Welfare

We have described how patronage democracy, political society, party politics, and social mobilization from below constitute different and important ways of understanding why citizens in some parts of India are suffering more or less than others.

Another way of thinking about welfare is through a tipping point model of ideational development that was alluded to in earlier chapters. A tipping point model can be contrasted with a punctuated equilibrium model. In the punctuated equilibrium model, an exogenous shock changes the trajectory of domestic institutions. For example, Acemoglu and Robinson (2012) argue that it was the benevolent features of British colonialism that engendered liberal values and property rights that set the stage for modern economic development. North America, thanks to its British legacy, thus produced a kind of prosperity that we did not find in South America. This story is akin to the impact of a meteor—a relatively short-run but powerful exogenous shock produced a long-term change in the trajectory of development.

The tipping point model, on the other hand, is akin to an earthquake model of path dependent change. This is more like the shift of tectonic plates that takes place over a long period of time and when pressures build up to a critical mass—change that is fairly continuous, but appears discontinuous. The exogenous shock in this story is less significant than endogenous changes in ideas. I have argued elsewhere and in another chapter that this argument works for understanding the transition to the big bang industrial deregulation and globalization of 1991. What appeared to be discontinuous change favouring globalization and deregulation in 1991, was driven largely by a movement of ideas in the domestic realm. The reason why India did not favour globalization and deregulation in 1966 but opted for it in 1991 was the weight of the internal policy consensus favouring deregulation in 1991 that did not exist in 1966. Is this logic of change also relevant for comprehending the three iconic measures favouring citizen well-being: the Mahatma Gandhi National Rural Employment Guarantee Act, the right to education and the right to information?

There are number of reasons why the idea that India's growth is not serving the poor had become quite widespread by 2004. That growth needs to become more inclusive was noted even by Montek Singh Ahluwalia in his Nehru Lecture delivered in April 2005. It must be noted that Ahluwalia has the reputation for being a growth-oriented technocrat. It had become clear to policymakers across the spectrum that while corporate India especially in the information technology sector was shining, agriculture which fed the vast majority of Indians was growing at snail's pace.

There were also electoral reasons for this change of heart. It is the poor who vote in India more than the rich. And, these poor people were demanding welfare in return for votes. The Congress Party had come to power in the 2004 elections in partnership with the CPM. This political alignment was a propitious moment for the politics of redistribution. There is statistical evidence to suggest that the welfare measures introduced by the Congress Party after 2005 had positive political gains for the party, even though the main reason for the success of the party in 2009 was the poor performance of its arch rival the BJP and a superb poll strategy. Democratic politics in India was perhaps reinforcing the logic of welfare in an era of rapid economic growth.

Mahatma Gandhi National Rural Employment Guarantee Scheme

Can we understand the initiation of the National Rural Employment Guarantee Act as an idea that legitimized guaranteeing employment to the poor which tipped over the belief that the needy should be left to their own devices for securing employment in 2005? This is one of the largest employment generation programs in the world, which if implemented properly should create 100 days of employment on demand for every Indian citizen in need of work. Work would be made available within 15 days of demand, failing which there is the provision of an employment allowance. This is a bottom-up demand-driven process where only those who seek hard manual labour receive work. The nature of work, which largely involves intensive digging, is shunned by people who can afford not to participate in it.

The Congress and the BJP had differing electoral agendas during the elections of 2004. While India was shining for the latter, it was not such a rosy economic scenario for the former. The Congress Party under-stood in 2004 upon being voted to power that it was not socially sustainable to pursue rapid economic growth when large sections of society were not ben-efiting from it. Growth was benefiting a few people in the service sector. Agriculture, which fed more than half the population, was growing very gradually and its share in India's GDP was declining rapidly. Rural employment, education, and health were therefore priorities for the new government.

How did the MGNREGS come about? The idea that every poor rural citizen has a right to be employed can provide social protection for the labouring classes from exploitation by rapacious landlords. More than 90 per cent of India's work force is not unionized. The right to employment was part of the directive principles of state policy but was not a justifiable right. This right therefore has a long legacy. Employment guarantees in rural areas had been a demand of the labour move-ment but there was no political groundswell favouring it. Scholars had noted the success of the Maharashtra Employment Guarantee Scheme, which paid equal wages to men and women. Women participating in this programme felt a sense of relief to be released from family and gained confidence by earning wages.

There had been no electoral groundswell of sup-port for the Act in 2005. Guaranteeing employment somehow became part of the Congress manifesto in 2004. The Congress Party realized that welfare would be good for the party and the electorate even though there was no compelling political reason to go ahead with the act in the immediate aftermath of the 2004 election. Members active in the National Advisory Committee (NAC) headed by Congress President Sonia Gandhi had been struggling for employment guarantees in Rajasthan. The NAC drafted an act but the National Rural Employment Guarantee Bill (2004) was a rather diluted version of that draft. It was the combined power of the NAC and the left parties that led to the passage of this Act on 23rd August 2005. The Act became operational since February 2006.

Sonia Gandhi helped to counter some provisions of the Act that were sought to be diluted by the Ministry of Rural Development. The People's Action for Employment Guarantees (PAEG), a diverse and loosely knit group of people involved with activism, non-governmental organizations, trade unions, and academic pursuits participated in this effort. But the Planning Commission and the Ministry of Finance were initially unsympathetic to the Act. Rapid economic growth and a rising tax to GDP ratio also helped to shoulder the financial implications of this act. In 2009–10 at Rs 40,000 crore ($8.65 billion) the scheme was consuming only 0.65 per cent of India's GDP.

National Rural Employment Guarantee Scheme (NREGS) implementation is a matter that varies from state to state. A recent study by Shankar, Gaiha, and Jha (2011) note the relative success of the MGNREGS in the state of Andhra Pradesh (AP). In 2010–11, AP created 3.1 million jobs whereas Maharashtra created 78,000 and Rajasthan about 595,000 jobs. While MGNREGS implementation is less than picture perfect in AP, it is important to consider why MGNREGS was more successful in the state. Another independent study published in the *Economic and Political Weekly* (2012) based on the National Sample Survey data collected in 2009–10 praised AP's effort at creating jobs through the MGNREGS.

Why was MGNREGS implemented so successfully in AP? Chief Minister Y.S. Rajashekhar Reddy should be credited with providing critical political support to a committed rural development bureaucracy. K. Raju, a socially committed IAS officer who is with the NAC was charged with heading a team of committed civil servants. Reddy had ensured that there would be no political interference with respect to MGNREGS at a time when large and middle farmers would be hit by the rise in wages of landless and marginal farmers.

It was known to him that poor implementation of former chief minister Chandrababu Naidu's food-for-work programme, which largely benefited the cadres of the Telugu Desam Party in AP, had not won him any political capital.

The architecture of MGNREGS in AP had some distinguishing characteristics. First, MGNREGS implementation would be directed by officials rather than by village governments (panchayats) because it was opined that panchayats are driven largely by the concerns of upper caste groups. Field officers appointed by the government rather than panchayats would decide what projects would go to which person in a village. Second, Tata Consultancy Services provided a transactions software free of cost to track MGNREGS related financial movements. This software has proved to be useful in tracking projects and funds.

Third, a social audit office was created within the government akin to a regulator of the programme. Funding for the social audit office came directly from MGNREGS funds. The person selected to head this office was a former MKSS activist with a degree in social work from the prestigious Tata Institute of Social Sciences in Mumbai. Sowmya Kidambi was known to be actively engaged in MKSS style social audit on behalf of the government. The governing Board had eminent social activists as members. Kidambi was constantly travelling from village to village meeting people in public hearings. Corrupt officials were sometimes forced to pay back the money that they had embezzled. Rs 17 crores had been retrieved as corruption money during the process of social audit in December 2011. Rs 125 crores worth of embezzlement had been reported. A senior IAS official overseeing rural development in the state reported that the government was attempting to give the social audit procedure the status of a criminal court. Corruption was rampant in AP but the jobs of 8,000 corrupt officials had also been terminated. Social audit was effective and swift, though also an imperfect way of dealing with corruption.

Finally, a number of NGOs funded by the government were training workers in the area of rights. These NGOs would typically be given Rs 500 per training session for educating 20 potential workers about their rights within MGNREGS. It was well understood that a rights based approach to development depended on how citizens viewed their rights. The need for worker training had led to a proliferation of NGOs run by educated middle class living in the villages and small towns in AP.

The most interesting corruption story during my trip to AP in December 2011–January 2012 was narrated by MGNREGS workers in the village of Upparahal in Kurnool district in AP. I was taken to this work site by a representative of the NGO Rural Development Initiatives. Workers pointed me to a canal sanctioned for approximately Rs 382,000 which was supposed to employ 3,009 workers at the rate of Rs 102 per day. This canal was all but missing when I reached the site on 19 December 2011. Had the canal been constructed as pointed out in the official papers, it would have crossed a tarred road and would have cut through the middle of a person's farm land. The project was clearly not in the interest of farmers and what existed on paper was nowhere to be seen on the ground. Moreover, the government official taking care of MGNREGS in this village had no valid answers about accusations made by these villagers.

Corruption was therefore rampant in Upparahal. One could guess the extent of corruption in a village by the ease with which one could access the muster rolls documenting workers and their wages. Many villages updated the muster rolls painted on village walls. One could go to a villager and check what was in the books or pasted on the wall. Corruption was rampant despite these measures in varying degrees in various villages. Many villagers complained that the smart card project implemented by AXIS Bank which helped workers obtain the full wage amount in some parts of AP was delayed in most areas. In the present form of payment through a post office, the post master in the local post office often took a cut from the wages. The villagers were keen to reduce their dependence on the post office and receive smart cards as soon as possible. The villagers of Upparahal were outspoken and did not seem to fear the field officer who must have sanctioned a project that could have only been consumed by corruption.

Was all the sanctioned money being pocketed by officials in Upparahal? I found that the complaining villagers of Upparahal belonging largely to dalit or backwards caste groups (about 30 in number) were nevertheless earning about Rs 500 per week on average. Interviews in Upparahal and other villages in Kurnool and Anantapur districts suggested that the poor and landless were benefiting from MGNREGS in AP. Landlords were being forced to pay a higher wage during the harvest season. Seasonal migration to Bengaluru and the vegetable farms of Guntur district in AP during the lean season had become much less frequent in all the villages I visited. Stable family life was conducive for educating children in these rural parts of India. I found poor landless peasants sending their girl children to cheap local private schools rather than the free but largely non-performing government schools.

The veteran social activist N.S. Bedi of the Young India Project took me and my colleague Sujoy Dutta to a fascinating work site near the village of Upparawanka in Anantapur district. This is one of the poorest districts in the country. Workers at this site were unionized by the local leader Narayana. He led the struggle to fire a corrupt village level technical assistant who was earlier executing the projects in the village. Unionized workers were paying a fee to the union to ensure that their rights be protected. About 80 per cent of the workers at this site were women, who were earning between Rs 70 and 120 per day depending on the amount of work delivered. Work at these sights was hard manual digging work. Approximately 40 per cent of the workers carried cell phones. Migration to Bengaluru during the non-harvest season had been reduced and the children of these workers were going to schools. Narayana's work on the ground was so productive that a senior politician had sought his help for garnering votes during the previous state-level elections in AP. It would be a welcome development if welfare measures such as MGNREGS rather than patronage becomes the reason for garnering votes.

It was a matter of concern, however, that most of the workers were women. While women's participation is clearly a sign of development, could it be that while women were working, men were becoming lazier? There were usual complaints about men getting drunk. But most women seemed to control their wages at Upparawanka.

A recent survey in the *Economic and Political Weekly* (2012) using 2009–10 data obtained from the National Sample Survey provides a fairly positive assessment of MGNREGS. First, poorer states are generally demanding more work although a few of them are not. States with a high proportion of citizens living below the poverty line like Chhattisgarh, Jharkhand, Madhya Pradesh, and West Bengal are demanding substantial work but other poor ones such as Bihar, Jharkhand, and Orissa are not. The demand for work in Chhattisgarh is five times that of Bihar even though the poverty rate is the same in both the states. Second, even though local social power relations affected the availability of work in some states, this is not a national level pattern. This implies that self-targeting through demand for hard manual labour seems to be largely at work. The requirement of hard manual labour is a security against elite capture of the scheme. Finally, women's partici-pation rate in MGNREGS is about twice the same in casual wage work, even though there is substantial variation among states.

This account of MGNREGS points towards a tip-ping point model of citizen empowering economic change. The idea that the rural poor had a right to livelihood gained prominence in 2004. It was rein-forced by the electoral debacle of the BJP that year. India shining had lost its sheen and the need for citizen concern and redistribution had been reinforced by the electoral outcome. Ultimately, MGNREGS also paid off electorally. The arrival of a major employment generation programme in India was not an externally induced economic programme. CSDS data suggested that programs like the MGNREGS may have played a positive role in the Congress Party's in getting re-elected in 2009.

The Right to Education

A similar case for the tipping point can be made about the enactment of the Right to Education Act enacted in 2009. Any scholar hoping to uncover India's journey from a stratified society that justified child labour in the name of poverty, to one where almost all children were going to school, needs to dwell on the movement of ideas that capture the imagination of governments. It was not the poor who first demanded education. The state had emphasized the primacy of higher education over primary education for a long time. This was clear-ly reflected in the dismal investments committed by the Government of India towards primary education. Myron Weiner's (1979) ethnographic account of child workers travelling to Sivakasi in Tamil Nadu in the mid-1980s who met with an accident tells the story of government's apathy towards literacy rather well. It was in the interest of the match makers of Sivakasi to employ child workers and control production costs.

When a senior government official discovered that laws were being violated in Sivakasi—he recommended that children should be given better work conditions rather than be sent to school. Otherwise, it would be difficult for Indian match makers to compete with the Swedish manufacturers WIMCO which was using machines rather than children.

Given the legacy of government neglect towards children coming from poor families, India's performance in higher education has surpassed its achievements in primary and secondary education. Its famed Indian Institutes of Technology, the All India Institute of Medical Sciences, the Indian Institutes of Management, the Indian Institute of Science, the Tata Institute of Fundamental Research, the Jawaharlal Nehru University and a number of research institutions have boosted India's status as a knowledge economy. Some of these institutions have served the information technology sector. India has exported doctors and professionals to the US who have made for a powerful and wealthy Indian diaspora. But India's literacy rate is only 74 per cent when the same figures for Sri Lanka and China exceed 90 per cent.

The journey towards the right to education is the saga of the state's belated realization that it had not expended substantial effort in getting all its children to schools. Moreover, the state had to deal with the politically powerful groups that benefited from cheap labour available in the form of children. Prime Minister Indira Gandhi realized that the central government needed to play a more decisive role in education. The constitution was suitably amended in 1976, and education was shifted from the state to the concurrent list of the Indian Constitution. This was essential to initiate central government sponsored schemes at the state level.

Prime Minister Rajiv Gandhi's National Policy on Education and the National Literacy Mission were to make India literate on a mission mode. India needed to expend more financial resources to get all its children into schools. In 1993, the Supreme Court highlighted this idea and linked the right to education to the right to life, which was guaranteed under the Indian Constitution. Later, the same court ordered the mid-day meal programme that had successfully promoted literacy in Tamil Nadu to become a nationwide programme. Poor parents now had greater incentives to send their children to school—at least this would assure their children a free meal. This was followed by the Sarva Shiksha Abhiyan or the Education for All programme launched by the BJP government in 2001. It is this movement of thought and action that ultimately produced the Right to Education in 2009.

The Right to Education Act was a tipping point that had been reached after decades of hard work. It had built on the legacy of the Education for All Programme initiated by the BJP, which moved literacy closer to the status of a right. From now on, it would be illegal to keep a child away from school. That it took till 2009 to obtain this right for every citizen demonstrates the substantial oppositional interests ranged against this enactment. Every child now has a right to be educated and it is illegal to deprive a child of this right. 25 per cent of the seats in private schools have been reserved for the poor. This right would affect vested interests in industry that had benefited from child labour. Middle class households would worry about losing cheap labour for household work. The right also needed to overcome the expectation among poor families that children are an economic asset because they comprise more earning members within a family. Finally, it had to fight the prejudice within government that if all children were educated, where would the jobs come from? Fortunately, economic growth and globalization seem to be demanding a better educated and healthier work force. Indian policymakers who were earlier worried about an over populated workforce now talk about the harnessing India's demographic dividend.

The movement of the idea from literacy as the exclusive preserve of the middle class to a public service that should be accessed by all has not resolved all the problems of primary education in India. The quality of government schooling is poor and the child drop-out rate is worrisome in many parts of the country. These require substantial effort on the part of governments. The rise of this idea within the government has spurred the literacy movement in India aided by non-governmental organizations. India's literacy rate has jumped from 61 per cent to 74 per cent between 2001 and 2011, and almost all of India's children were going to school in 2011. Unfortunately, many of India's older illiterate citizens will be never become literate. The challenge for India has more to do with improving the quality of government schools than sending all children to school.

Right to Information (RTI)

A right based approach to development in a poverty stricken democracy can hardly help marginalized citizens if they did not know how their rights were being violated. The poorest of the poor may have the right to work and a minimum wage. The government may sanction public works in rural areas to create employment. What if the village headman siphons off this money for personal and political consumption by naming workers who were either dead or had migrated from the location? Such public works enrich the local politician at the cost of the poor on whom the government had invested. Similarly, there may be a right to education but a school that was committed may not have even been constructed. Or, the school may have fewer amenities than what was committed and paid for. Information is vital for securing the rights of all citizens—rich and poor.

This section will elaborate how an ideational tipping point was reached based on civic action and social movements. This is a classic saga of how slow moving social processes accumulate a certain momentum up to a point when a political opportunity can be exploited to transact what looks like a rather discontinuous change. What appears to be a major shift is driven largely by internal processes over time rather than being externally imposed or a sheer conjecture.

How did the idea of secrecy enshrined in the Official Secrets Act (1923) get replaced with the idea that transparent governance is vital for serving Indian citizens? Opposition to this idea came from a variety of quarters and was expressed in a number of ways. Those opposed to public disclosure of government information argued that access to information would hamper the work of the government. Civil servants were likely to become rule bound and would not use discretion because this could be construed as favouritism. They needed to make quick imperfect decisions because sometimes time is of the essence. Such quick decisions would be jeopardized. Civil servants would now have the incentive to play to the galleries rather than taking a tough decision that could displease some people. Moreover, vested interests would use the act to blackmail civil servants and create delays.

Though RTI has not revolutionized welfare provisioning in India, it is indeed a perceptible and gradual evolutionary process that is transforming citizens' ways of dealing with governments. The social movement towards the right to information was a gradual process that was supported by courts and social activists. The MKSS played a crucial role in mobilizing people towards that effort. Their technique of a public hearing in a village to shame local officials to make them pay back corrupt earning had mobilized the people of Rajasthan. Political mobilization positively contributed to convincing governments about the efficacy of this right for welfare provision in India. This social activism tipped towards a powerful act in 2005, aided by successful social experiments and engagement with professionals, civil servants, lawyers, and the media.

People's movements working on economic rights such as minimum wages, human rights, and environmental rights all converged to the view that the right to privileged information was essential if the Indian state had to be made accountable to its citizens. In this respect, the formation of the MKSS played a powerful role in the struggle for obtaining information.

The movement was pioneered by three idealistic individuals who had decided to work among the people of a village named Devdungri in a poor, illiterate, and drought-prone part of Rajasthan. Aruna Roy had resigned from her job with the IAS in 1987. Nikhil Dey left higher studies in the US to join Roy. And, Shankar Singh who was from a nearby local village played the role of grounding the movement in the soil of Rajasthan. Inspired by Gandhian ideals, these three persons spent considerable time in the village exploring local problems in the village. They wished to live simply like the people of Devdungri, identify the problems bottom-up living with these people, and, help them realize their basic rights. The idea was not so much to demand something new but to ensure that the rights guaranteed under the Constitution benefited the citizens of India living in Devdungri. Representative democracy had to be strengthened with participatory development. Moreover, the group would be political but would remain above the fray of party politics. It was during their struggles, especially for obtaining minimum wages that the participants of the movement realized the importance of information. The value of information and its subversion would not easily be lost to Roy because she had spent years on the side of the government as a member of the elite IAS. MKSS was thus born on 1 May 1990.

The MKSS perfected the instrument of 'jan sunwai' or public hearing as a way of discovering corruption that hurt the poorest workers and peasants. In a public hearing pertaining to minimum wages in a government development scheme, information about expenditures would first be obtained. Thereafter the people of the village participating in the scheme would be invited to corroborate facts. These public hearings soon established how funds were being siphoned-off to various parties in the name of the poor. It was found that a large number of people who were either dead or had migrated or were non-existent were the supposed beneficiaries of these programs. And, many of those paid for their labour received less than the minimum wage. When such data became public, rural folk in Rajasthan began to support such initiatives in large numbers.

Substantial effort was required to obtain this information protected under the Official Secrets Act (1923). However, there were progressive sympathizers of this social movement even within the government. When one district collector—the top IAS official in the district—gave instructions to issue photocopies of muster rolls pertaining to public works, bill, and vouchers, the village level development officers failed to comply with the orders of the collector and went on strike. This opposition from local level development officials notwithstanding, the public hearings of MKSS revealed the state of corruption in this particular village. The detailed findings were presented to the collector. When a government official arrived at Bagmal village, 24 village heads displayed their displeasure about the complaining villagers in no uncertain terms. A woman sarpanch (village head-woman) even tore the shirt of a complaining farmer. It is significant that the local administration in the four districts where MKSS was active, refused to register criminal cases against the officials, despite substantial evidence provided by villagers. Concrete evidence of corruption in the form of government documents was essential for fighting corruption. Nevertheless, the people's mobilization spearheaded by a few idealistic Gandhians was gaining momentum.

The social movement favouring disclosure of information was gaining momentum. In October 1995, the chief minister of Rajasthan declared in the state legislature that his government would be the first in the country to make available all documents pertaining to development projects. When the chief minister could not make good his promise within a year, MKSS launched a protest in the small town of Beawar, pressing for the right to information about public documents. The government responded by allowing citizens to inspect the documents for a fee but did not allow them to photocopy these documents. This was unacceptable to MKSS. This movement generated widespread support that cut across class and religion. Rich shopkeepers, professionals, and daily wage workers—all supported the movement for transparency and provided financial and moral support. The movement then spread from Beawar to Jaipur around May 1996 and attracted the attention of many organizations working for civic rights. The government issued a press note during the same month detailing its commitment to transparency and formed a committee that would fulfil the pledge of the chief minister. When there was no action for a year, another protest was launched in May 1997. In an astonishing deception after 52 days of protest the deputy chief minister of Rajasthan announced that the government had notified the right to receive photocopies of documents related to village level local governments. This was a milestone. One wondered why such a notification had been hidden from the public's gaze.

MKSS's efforts had won sympathizers within government. This link with the progressive bureaucracy benefited the right to information movement. In October 1995, the Lal Bahadur Shastri National Academy of Administration charged with the task of training civil servants in India held a national workshop on the right to information. This effort was backed by socially committed officers within the administrative service whose efforts to empower citizens were largely unrealized because of the dearth of institutions protecting the poor against corrupt elites in power.

There are numerous examples of civil servants whose attempts to serve citizens were thwarted by the absence of appropriate transparency laws. To give just one example: a socially committed commissioner in Madhya Pradesh sought to introduce transparent mechanisms in the public distribution of foodgrains meant for the poor at a subsidized price. The records of food stocks were to be made available at the local tehsil office and photocopies of these records could be accessed by all. Vigilance over the stocks was to check the diversion of subsidized foodgrains to the open market. Likewise, the employment exchange was to share details about hiring criteria and processes in the district. And, the pollution control board was required to collect and report data on pollutants in daily newspapers. These measures improved governance during the period when the officer administered the district. But local power elites had the officer transferred. Thereafter, the district was back to the old days. Secrecy had beneficiaries who were more powerful than the protagonists of transparency.

The example above highlighted that India's democracy needed to empower officers who were waging a war on corruption. These officials would support any move striving for transparency and citizen welfare. The National Campaign for People's Right to Information (NCPRI) was born in a meeting convened at the Gandhi Peace Foundation in New Delhi in 1996. This was a meeting point for activists, lawyers, journalists, retired civil servants, and academics who played a critical role in strategizing the struggle for the right to information. The NCPRI drafted a right to information bill that was sent to Justice S.B. Sawant—the chairperson of the Press Council of India. Justice Sawant was a retired judge of the Supreme Court. The Council suggested amendments to the bill. The revised draft bill was presented in various conferences in New Delhi and drew widespread support across the political spectrum.

Armed with a draft bill the NCPRI approached the United Front government (1996) which was a shaky anti-Congress coalition of parties. Anti-Congress governments in power between 1977–9 and 1989–90 had earlier discussed the need for such a bill. The United Front government set up a committee headed by H.D. Shourie to look into the matter in 1996. According to one view, the tyranny of a committee can be quite debilitating with proponents of secrecy gaining the upper hand over those who favour transparency in the dealings of the government. Subsequently, BJP came to power in 1998. In 1999, Cabinet Minister Ram Jethmalani ordered that all files in his ministry be opened to public scrutiny—an injunction that was overturned by Prime Minister Vajpayee. This was a substantial opening for activists struggling for transparency, especially because eminent lawyer and Law Minister Jethmalani's action was consistent with various earlier judgments of the Supreme Court. Moreover, weak RTI laws had been legislated in states such as Tamil Nadu, Goa, Madhya Pradesh, Maharashtra, Karnataka, Rajasthan, Assam, Jammu and Kashmir, and Delhi before the Act was passed by the Parliament in New Delhi.

This legislative momentum favouring an RTI Act became difficult for the government to ignore. A Supreme Court judgment gave an ultimatum to the government in 2002 to pass an act in response to a petition before the court. The Freedom of Information Act was consequently passed during the same year. This Act though passed in Parliament was never notified, signalling a temporary victory of those who favoured secrecy.

The movement favouring the right to information had reached a tipping point building on a history struggles favouring transparency. These largely endogenous social processes were now aided by the assent of the Congress Party to power in May 2004 as the leading party in the United Progressive Alliance (UPA) coalition government. The common minimum programme of the government promised transparency and accountability in governance. The NAC was to monitor the common minimum programme of the coalition government. NCPRI exploited this rare opportunity with a revised bill which would be more citizen friendly than the Freedom of Information Act. Deliberations between the Council and the Prime Minister led to the introduction of the Freedom of Information Bill in December 2004. The bill was more citizen friendly than the earlier act but it concerned only the central government. State governments had escaped from this legislation. This feature of the bill could have a debilitating impact on citizen welfare because the citizen met the state most frequently in the states of the Indian union. Finally, the Group of Ministers headed by Pranab Mukherjee was success-fully lobbied and the RTI Act was passed in Parliament in May 2005. It became fully operational in the month of October the same year.

The threats to disclosure did not end here. There arose differences in opinion with regard to whether file noting by the executive in government files fell within the purview of the act. A file noting on an executive decision can reveal a lot about a minister or a civil servant's view on a particular policy issue. President Abdul Kalam had wished that file noting and communication between the President and Prime Minister be kept beyond the purview of this act. But the right to access such information was protected under the RTI Act. Only information vital for national security could be secured exclusively within the confines of the Indian state. Given the alert nature of activists bent on securing the right, subsequent attempts to keep file noting beyond the purview of the Act through an amendment, also failed to pass muster.

Paradoxically enough, the office of the Chief Justice of India too wished to remain above the purview of the Act. The Supreme Court, which had supported activists in their quest to secure this right dithered in supporting the Act when it came to the disclosure of its own affairs. This move too was unsuccessful, largely because of the efforts of activists who convinced the Chairperson of the UPA and the NAC—Sonia Gandhi—about double standards involved with such an amendment of the RTI Act.

The RTI Act is a powerful weapon in the hands of an alert citizenry. Much of the material on the infamous 2G telecom scam (January 2008) was made available through the act to crusaders such as Subramaniam Swamy. The act enabled citizens to trace files between

Telecommunications Minister A. Raja, the Finance Minister P. Chidambaram and Prime Minister Manmohan Singh. Such information provided citizens a rare glimpse of how the government can get corrupted by the machinations of certain ministers due to the compulsions of coalition politics. Such is the power of the act that the government seems to be ridden with excessive corruption because more information is available in the public domain. News channels such as NDTV have inaugurated awards for those who used the act to expose corruption. There is now a need to physically protect crusaders favouring democratic rights from the powerful few whom the Official Secrets Act (1923) had protected in the past.

The act has made an impact on the Indian citizen. In 2008, the Department of Personnel, Government of India, commissioned a report on the status of implementation of the right to information to PricewaterhouseCoopers (PwC). Civil society organizations also conducted a larger nation-wide survey. Both came to similar conclusions. The awareness about RTI was still low. This was especially so among rural women. The people's survey found that out of two million applications filed 400,000 came from rural areas.

More than half the rural applicants and greater than 40 per cent of the urban applicants did not have an undergraduate degree. RTI had thus become a handy tool in the hands of citizens who did not have high connections in government. It was an even more effective weapon in the hands of the educated citizenry.

★ ★ ★

The level of citizen well-being continues to be a matter of grave concern in India. Indian politics is ridden with caste-based patronage. Political parties are often willing to make concessions in return for votes but not grant members of political society their rights as citizens. These facets of Indian democracy have the propensity to delay the process of making the government accountable to its citizens.

There is room for hope, however. First, this hope arose from political parties with a pro-poor or backward caste social base which had the propensity to deliver basic services to citizens. The CPM in West Bengal in the late 1970s and the early 1980s and the DMK and the AIADMK parties in Tamil Nadu are two such parties. These experiences reveal the importance of the relationship between the social base of the governing parties and developmental outcomes. We need to know more about the conditions under which backward caste parties turn away from populism and exclusively caste based political patronage towards citizen well-being. It would help these parties that the poorer people have more faith in Indian democracy and are voting more frequently than the richer ones in India.

Second, hope also arises from social movements such as the one led by MKSS that have sought to reach constitutional guarantees to the citizens of India. Such social movements clearly arouse the electorate and help to convince governments about the presence of citizens in a democracy. MKSS's struggles in Rajasthan made an impact both on the state and the central government as it sought to bring legislation on the right to information.

The missing link in this development debate is the role of ideas. This chapter has demonstrated that no matter how robust India's democracy, the gradual evolution of ideas up to a tipping point was essential for citizen well-being in many areas. Social movements can help but not until the political class is convinced about the goals pursued by these movements. Moreover, these social movements are also led by norm entrepreneurs who mobilize people on the ground because they believe that citizens have certain rights. This conviction evolves gradually over time and cannot be understood merely on the basis of the interests of the ruling class. It is important to chart the political and social processes that make these ideas momentous and bring them to a tipping point when a political opening such as change in political dispensation with sympathizers can bring about transitions that look quite discontinuous from the past. What looks discontinuous from the past is quite path dependent. The right to information, the right to education and the right to employment are three important pillars of citizen well-being that traversed such a path. It would be interesting to see whether these rights will make an impact on the Indian citizen's right to food and health as well.

4

Reflecting on
Economic Reforms

The politics and economics that produced economic
policy and institutions in India were different from
those which emerged in many parts of the post-
colonial and developing world. Communist countries
abolished private property and did not participate
in trade because it was viewed as an impediment to
egalitarian development. The US allies in Europe and
Asia, on the other hand, embraced trade and foreign
investment as a path to development. Trade-led growth
lifted billions of people out of poverty and persuaded
China to follow a similar path. India's political economy steered a course between these two extremes.
We find that politics played a central role in shaping
India's development.

India's has been a middling third way between aggressive economic globalization and private sector promotion, and totally self-sufficient, state-controlled development. Neither could India give up the ideal of socialism, nor could it abolish private property even when the most radical economic ideas inhabited the policy space. The extent and significance of private property varied over time. The state was substantially in command between 1956 and 1974 and gradually began deregulating after 1975. The period beyond 1975 found the government criticizing previous policies and gradually deregulating the economy. Economic growth and poverty alleviation picked up in the 1980s and furthermore after 1991. The changes in ideas and policies since the mid-1970s led to a paradigm shift in policies in 1991, when the government took advantage of a crisis to change the very assumptions that drove economic policies in India. India had made a rather dramatic shift from state-led import substitution to economic deregulation and globalization in 1991—a policy and institutional path that would get reinforced in the forthcoming decades.

We find ideas within government to be of substantial importance during the defining moments for

India's economic trajectory. State-directed import substitution set the tone for India's economic policies in
the mid-1950s. These policies can be explained largely
by the way in which Prime Minister Nehru and his
economic advisors viewed good policies rather than
by the interests of the business class. In the mid-1950s,
about half a decade after the death of India's powerful deputy Prime Minister Sardar Patel, Nehru man-
aged to create a policy hegemonic environment. He
could fashion Indian planning in a manner that was
neither liked by politically powerful rich farmers, nor
was particularly pleasing to Indian industrialists who
subsequently adjusted rather comfortably to the new
policy environment.

Similarly we find that economic ideas held within
the government were particularly important in 1991—
the year India witnessed a defining paradigm shift from
autarkic state-control to economic globalization and
deregulation. This shift was more due to an internal
consensus at the time of a Balance of Payment (BoP)
crisis than an imposition from the International
Monetary Fund (IMF). The IMF was a lender of the
last resort under these circumstances. The business
class' dependence on the IMF for foreign exchange

helped the government deal with vested interests within Indian industry who desired status quo because these industrialists desperately needed foreign exchange for imports when the country had financial reserves that could finance only two weeks of imports. Indian industrialists were the beneficiaries of high levels of protection and preferential access to industrial and import licenses, and had enjoyed production monopolies in India. The government exploited this moment of dependence of the Indian business class on the IMF for foreign exchange to transform economic institutions.

India had faced a similar crisis in 1966 when a different set of ideas produced vastly different policy outcomes. When the dominant ideas of the time favoured state-control and import substitution—the government made a temporary retreat by devaluing the Indian Rupee—only to practice the most stringent version of import substitution after 1967.

How did India's economic institutions change? Comparative literature has noted that India is a relatively weak state surrounded by powerful actors. Despite this relative weakness of the state, the political economy of change in India depended to a large extent on how the government thought. We demonstrated how new policy ideas arose when old ideas failed to deliver desired benefits. Challenges to old ideas evolved gradually and reached a tipping point after reaching a critical mass. We have noted that the tipping point resembles an earthquake rather than a meteor. Endogenous slow-moving changes are important in the earthquake model. What appears an abrupt discontinuous change is largely the result of gradual endogenous forces rather than a meteor-like external short-term impact which produces long-term transformation in institutional paths. A meteor-like impact would be an externally induced IMF imposition of policies and institutions which create a long-term change in institutional paths. India's responses to financial crises in 1966 and 1991 demonstrate that external impositions are a largely futile endeavour in India.

Rights-based institutional changes promoting welfare also seem to be following a similar tipping point path. The right to employment in India was legislated based on the view that economic growth notwithstanding, India was not shining for everybody. This was a powerful idea that built on the previous experiences of anti-poverty programs. The Maharashtra Employment

161

Guarantee Scheme was the most immediate inspiration for the National Rural Employment Guarantee Act (NREGA). The United Progressive Alliance (UPA) government with the support of the left legislated NREGA (2005), which is landmark legislation despite many shortcomings in implementation.

The right to information (RTI) followed a similar tipping point in its evolution. This act (2005) transformed the normative basis of government institutions based on official secrecy to ones premised on accountability and transparency. It is the mother of the rights-based approach to development because it has the capacity to check grand and petty corruption. The struggles of the Mazdoor Kisan Shakti Sangathan (MKSS or the Organization for the Empowerment of Labourers and Farmers) in Rajasthan led by three remarkable individuals, yielded information on government corruption. Its leader Aruna Roy had resigned from the Indian Administrative Service to pursue activism and had excellent connections within government and civil society. These struggles led largely by the elite were taking place within and outside government. Subsequently, the new UPA government in 2004 founded the National Advisory Council (NAC) headed by the President of the Congress Party—Sonia Gandhi. Aruna Roy was invited to be part of it. The NAC and the government legislated a powerful act in 2005 with substantial potential for great transformation. It has been deployed to punish corrupt village headmen and cabinet ministers alike. The legislation is especially timely when deregulation of the economy has generated substantial potential for rent-seeking.

The Right to Education Act (2009) follows a similar evolutionary logic as well. Gradual policy and legislative changes occurred in the normative basis of dealing with literacy—from one which was premised on the idea that poor people's children should help their parents, to a view that illiteracy engenders poverty and has to be eradicated. The old view was largely challenged within the government. If 2009 constituted the tipping point for radical institutional change favouring literacy—it was preceded by measures like the National Literacy Mission, the Sarva Shiksha Abhiyan (Education for All Programme) and legislations which moved the institutions closer to a full-fledged right in 2009. Slow moving policy processes driven by ideational change within government were therefore critical for engendering institutional change.

The view that economic ideas, especially those held by the elite and the dominant ideas within government matter—does not imply that interests of powerful groups within society do not matter. We find that the powerful more often than not have an interest in maintaining the status quo. Rich farmers oppose a decent minimum wage. Powerful industrialists with stakes in import substitution oppose deregulation and globalization. The middle class, industrialists, and rich farmers—all have an interest in exploiting children for commercial work. Middle class workers oppose the unionization of the vast majority of the poor in the unorganized sector in order to protect their privileges.

We find that powerful interest groups have promoted both populism and citizen concern. Ethnically-based backward caste mobilization has produced symbolic gains for politically powerful ethnic groups in states such as Bihar and Uttar Pradesh. However a similar mobilization has produced genuine welfare in Tamil Nadu where backward caste mobilizations produced benefits for all citizens. The state has an excellent record in distributing food, implementing the National Rural Employment Guarantee Scheme, and in providing meals for children attending primary school. Similarly, the early years of rule by the Communist Party of India (Marxist) (CPI[M]) in the state of West Bengal had produced welfare because a cadre-based pro-poor party distributed land to the poor based on class rather than ethnic considerations.

Even though economic policies shaping growth and welfare have been shaped to a great extent by home-grown ideas, external context was important for the success of India's economic globalization. We find trade, aid, and security considerations to be interrelated. It would not have been easy for India to embrace economic globalization, had the Soviet Union not collapsed. The US is the largest consumer of India's booming service trade which has earned it the title—'the back-office of the world'. The country would not part with sensitive technology, nor sign a deal on commerce in nuclear materials and technology as long as India enjoyed special security and economic relations with the Soviet Union. India's successful 'Look East' policy was also premised on its ties with the US. Relations with American allies and friends in Southeast and East Asia improved radically only after the fall of the Berlin Wall. These commercial relations were critical for India's exports and imports after the country embraced a strategy of economic globalization after 1991.

The effect of the end of Cold War on South Asian economic integration was not equally evident, though. Indo-Pakistan rivalry has inhibited commercial relations in South Asia. Trade with Bangladesh and Sri Lanka could improve if these countries did not feel vulnerable with respect to India. Though the free trade agreement between India and Sri Lanka benefited from India's improved security relations with the country, there is still no agreement on service trade. Also, commercial relations with the country are below potential. India's trade with the city state of Singapore is larger than its entire trade with the South Asian region. That India's trade with its South Asian neighbours is less than 5 per cent of its total trade has more to do with geopolitics than economics. The good news is that India's growth is increasingly more appealing to its neighbours. If the country continues to grow and appear to be less threatening to its neighbours as well, regional economic integration could bring prosperity to one of the most poverty-stricken regions on the globe.

Substantial challenges to development remain despite the slow-moving processes that brought India to the tipping point of growth and rights-based welfare. An economy in deregulation mode needs powerful and effective regulators, who promote competition and check the excesses of private and public sector monopolists. Big business can bribe the government to extract favours because powerful industrialists are more interested in protecting their market-share through regulatory privileges than competing with other good companies. India's dismal record in physical and human infrastructure does not augur well for the production process. Moreover, a citizenry that is only 74 per cent literate, with an overwhelming majority malnourished cannot easily fight for its right to information, employment, and literacy. Moreover health and sanitary conditions in India remain deplorable. That India has grown despite these challenges is quite remarkable. There is still a long way to go for the country to overcome these challenges, and to make the growth path sustainable, as well as redistribute the benefits of that growth to a larger number of Indians. If the benefits of growth are limited to a few, the process will not be sustainable within democratic politics—which is now increasingly making demands for bottom-up development. Pressures from below are important for growth and welfare because welfare is ultimately quite heavily dependent on growth.

References

Acemoglu, D. and J.A. Robinson. 2012. *Why Nations Fail*. New York: Crown Business.

————. 2006. *Economic Origins of Dictatorship and Democracy*. New York: Cambridge University Press.

Aggarwal, V.K. and R. Mukherji. 2008. 'Shifts in India's Trade Policies: South Asia and Beyond', in V.K. Aggarwal and M. Gyo Koo (eds), *Asia's New Institutional Architecture*, pp. 215–59. Heidelberg: Springer.

Ahluwalia, M.S. 2007a. 'Economic Reforms in India Since 1991: Has Gradualism Worked?', in R. Mukherji (ed.), *India's Economic Transition*, pp. 27–51. New Delhi: Oxford University Press.

Ahluwalia, Montek S. 2007b. 'India in a Globalizing World', in B.R. Nayar (ed.), *Globalization and Politics in India*, pp. 199–217, New Delhi: Oxford University Press.

Aiyar, Yamini. 2010. 'Invited Spaces, Invited Participation', *India Review*, 9(2), 204–26.

Alexander, P.C. (Chair). 1978. *Report of the Committee on Import-Export Policies and Procedures*. New Delhi: Ministry of Commerce.

Amsden, A. 1985. 'The State and Taiwan's Economic Development', in P. Evans, D. Rueschmeyer, and T. Skocpol (eds), *Bringing the State Back In*, pp. 78–106. New York: Cambridge University Press.

Bardhan, P. 1998. *The Political Economy of Development in India*. New Delhi: Oxford University Press.

Baru, S. 2006. *Strategic Consequences of India's Economic Performance*. New Delhi: Academic Foundation.

Bhagwati, J. and T.N. Srinivasan. 1975. *Foreign Trade Regimes and Economic Development: India*. New York: National Bureau of Economic Research.

Bhagwati, J. 1998. 'The Design of Indian Development', in I.J. Ahluwalia and I.M.D. Little (eds). *India's Economic Reforms and Development: Essays for Manmohan Singh*, pp. 23–39. New Delhi: Oxford University Press.

————. 2007. 'What Went Wrong?', in R. Mukherji (ed.). *India's Economic Transition*, pp. 27–51. New Delhi: Oxford University Press.

Bhattacharya, A.K. 2011. 'The Months that Changed India', *Business Standard*, Delhi edn, 2 July.

Bjorkman, J.W. 2008. 'Public Law 480 and the Policies of Self Help and Short Tether: Indo-American Relations, 1965–68', in L.I. Rudolph, and S.H. Rudolph (eds), *Making US Foreign Policy Towards South Asia*, pp. 359–424. Bloomington: Indiana University Press.

Chakravarty, S. (Chair). 1985. *Report of the Committee to Review the Working of the Monetary System*. New Delhi: Reserve Bank of India.

Chand, R., S.S. Raju, and L.M. Pandey. 2007. 'Growth Crisis in Indian Agriculture', *Economic and Political Weekly*, 42(26): 2528–33.

Chandra, K. 2004. *Why Ethnic Parties Succeed: Patronage and Ethnic Head Counts in India*. New York and New Delhi: Cambridge University Press.

Chatterjee, P. 2011. *Lineages of Political Society*. New York: Columbia University Press.

Chibber, V. 2003. *Locked in Place*. Princeton: Princeton University Press.

Chopra, D. 2011. 'Policy Making in India: A Dynamic Process of Statecraft', *Pacific Affairs*, 84(1): 89–107.

Choudhry, P.K., V.L. Kelkar, and V. Yadav. 2004. 'The Evolution of Home-Grown Conditionality in India', *Journal of Development Studies*, 40(6): 59–81.

Choudhury, N., J. Hammer, M. Kramer, K. Muralidharan, and F.H. Rogers. 2006. 'Missing in Action: Teacher and Health Worker Absence in Developing Countries', *Journal of Economic Perspectives*, 20(1): 91–116.

Cohen, J.B. 1955. 'India's Foreign Economic Policies', *World Politics*, 7(4): 546–71.

Corbridge, S., G. Williams, and M. Srivastava. 2005. *Seeing the State: Governance and Governmentality in India*. Cambridge and New York: Cambridge University Press.

Corbridge, S., J. Harriss, and C. Jeffrey. 2013. *India Today: Economy, Politics and Society*. Cambridge: Polity Press.

Cullather, N. 2007. 'Hunger and Containment: How India Became Important in US Cold War Strategy', *India Review*, 6(2): 59–90.

Dagli, V. (Chair). 1979. *Report of the Committee on Controls and Subsidies*. New Delhi: Ministry of Finance.

Das, G. 2002. *India Unbound*. New Delhi: Penguin Books.

Dash, K.C. 2008. *Regionalism and South Asia*. London: Routledge.

Datar, A.L. 1972. *India's Economic Relations with the USSR and Eastern Europe*. Cambridge: Cambridge University Press.

Deaton, A. and J. Dreze. 2007. 'Poverty and Inequality in India: A Re-examination', in B.R. Nayar (ed.), *Globalization and Politics in India*, pp. 408–57. New Delhi: Oxford University Press.

Dev, S.M. 2012. 'Policies for Raising Agricultural Growth and Productivity in India', *IGIDR Proceedings/Projects Series* PP-069-SMDI. Mumbai: Indira Gandhi Institute for Development Research.

Djurfeldt, G., V. Athreya, N. Jayakumar, S. Lindberg, A. Rajagopal, and R. Vidyasagar. 2008. 'Agrarian Change and Social Mobility in Tamil Nadu', *Economic and Political Weekly*, 43(45): 52–60.

Donaldson, R.H. 1974. *Soviet Policy Towards India*. Cambridge: Harvard University Press.

Dreze, J. 2010. 'Employment Guarantee and the Right to Work', in N.G. Jayal and P.B. Mehta (eds), *The Oxford*

Companion to Politics in India, pp. 510–18. New Delhi: Oxford University Press.

Dubash, N.K. and S.C. Rajan. 2001. 'Power Politics', *Economic and Political Weekly*, 36(35): 3367–90.

Dutta, P., R. Murgai, M. Ravallion and D. Van De Walle. 2012. 'Does India's Employment Guarantee Scheme Guarantee Employment?', *Economic and Political Weekly*, XLVII(16): 55–64.

Echeverri-Gent, J. 2007. 'Politics of Market Micro-Structure', in R. Mukherji (ed.), *India's Economic Transition*, pp. 328–58. New Delhi: Oxford University Press.

Evans, P. 1995. *Embedded Autonomy.* Princeton: Princeton University Press.

Forbes, N. 2002. 'Doing Business in India', in A. Krueger (ed.), *Economic Policy Reforms and the Indian Economy*, pp. 129–68. New Delhi: Oxford University Press.

Frankel, F. 2005. *India's Political Economy.* New Delhi: Oxford University Press.

Galbraith, J.K. 1969. *Ambassador's Journal.* New York: Paragon House.

Gandhi, I. 1985. *Selected Speeches and Writings–Volume 4, 1980/81.* New Delhi: Publications Division of the Ministry of Information and Broadcasting.

Ganguly, S. 2002. *Conflict Unending: India-Pakistan Tensions Since 1947.* New Delhi: Oxford University Press.

Ganguly, S. and R. Mukherji. 2011. *India Since 1980.* New York and New Delhi: Cambridge University Press.

Ghosh, M. 2008. 'India and Japan: Growing Synergy', *Asian Survey* 48(2): 282–302.

Gokarn, S. and R. Vaidya. 2004. 'The Automobile Components Industry', in S. Gokarn, A. Sen and R.R. Vaidya (eds), *The Structure of Indian Industry*, pp. 281–314. New Delhi: Oxford University Press.

Goldstein, A. 2008. 'The Internationalization of Indian Companies', CASI Working Paper Number 08-02. Philadelphia: University of Pennsylvania.

Gould, Stephen J. and Niles Eldridge. 1977. 'Punctuated Equilibria', *Paleontological Society*, 3(2): 115–51.

Goyal, A. 2012a. 'Explaining the Infrastructure Slowdown', *Businessline*, Delhi edn. 11 October.

—————. 2012b. 'The Future of Financial Liberalization in South Asia', *Asia Pacific Development Journal*, 19(1): 63–96.

Gudavarthy, A. (ed.). 2012. *Reframing Democracy and Agency in India*. London: Anthem Press.

Guha, R. 2010. *Makers of Modern India*. New Delhi: Penguin Books.

Guha Thakurta, P. 2004. 'Ideological Contradictions in an Era of Coalitions: Economic Policy Confusion in the Vajpayee Government', in B. Debroy and R. Mukherji (eds), *India: The Political Economy of Reforms*, pp. 81–116. New Delhi: Bookwell and Rajiv Gandhi Institute of Contemporary Studies.

Gupta, S. 1964. *India and Regional Integration in Asia*. Bombay: Asia Publishing House.

Hagerty, D.T. 2006. 'Are we Present at the Creation? Alliance Theory and Indo–US Strategic Convergence', in S. Ganguly, B. Shoup, and A. Scobel (eds), *US–Indian Strategic Cooperation: Into the 21st Century*, pp. 11–37. London: Routledge.

Haggard, S. 1990. *Pathways from the Periphery*. New York: Cornell University Press.

Harriss, J. 2006. *Power Matters: Essays in Institutions, Politics, and Society in India*. New Delhi: Oxford University Press.

Harriss, J., J. Jayaranjan, and K. Nagaraj. 2010. 'Land, Labour and Caste Politics in Rural Tamil Nadu in the 20th Century: Iruvelpattu (1916–2008)', *Economic and Political Weekly*, XLV(31): 47–61.

Hirschman, A.O. 1980. *National Power and the Structure of Foreign Trade*. Berkeley: University of California Press.

Huang, Y. 2010. *Capitalism with Chinese Characteristics*. New York: Cambridge University Press.

Hussain, A. Chair. 1984. *Report of the Committee on Trade Policy*. New Delhi: Ministry of Commerce.

Jaffrelot, C. 1998. *India's Silent Revolution: The Rise of Lower Castes in North India*. New York: Columbia University Press.

———. 2003. 'India's Look East Policy', *India Review*, 2(2): 35–68.

Jaishankar, S. 2012. *India and China: Fifty Years After*. Singapore: Institute of South Asian Studies Special Report, 23 November.

Jauhari, R.C. 1994. 'The American Quest for a Treaty of Commerce with India', in A.P. Rana (ed.), *Four Decades of Indo-US Relations*, pp. 213–30. New Delhi: Har Anand.

Jayal, N. G. and P. B. Mehta (ed.). 2010. *The Oxford Companion to Politics in India*. New Delhi: Oxford University Press.

Jayawardena, L. 1993. *Indo-Sri Lanka Economic Cooperation*. Helsinki: The United Nations University—WIDER.

Jenkins, R. 1999. *Democratic Politics and Economic Reform in India*. Cambridge: Cambridge University Press.

Jenkins, R. and A.M. Goetz. 1999. 'Accounts and Accountability: Theoretical Implications of the Right-to-Information Movement in India', *Third World Quarterly*, 20(3): 603–22.

Joshi, V. and D. Kapur. forthcoming. 'India and the World Economy', in Delia Delvin and Barbara Harris-White (eds), *China-India: Path of Economic and Social Development*.

Kantha, S. and S. Ray. 2006. *Building India with Partnership: The Story of CII 1895–2005*. New Delhi: Penguin Books.

Kapur, D. 2002. 'The Causes and Consequences of India's IT Boom', *India Review*, 1(2): 93–102.

————. 2010. *Diaspora, Development and Democracy: The Domestic Impact of International Migration From India*. New Delhi: Oxford University Press.

Kapur, D. and P.B. Mehta (eds)). 2005. *Public Institutions in India*. New Delhi: Oxford University Press.

Kaviraj, S. 1997. 'A Critique of the Passive Revolution', in Partha Chatterjee (ed.), *State and Politics in India*. New Delhi: Oxford University Press.

Kelegama, S. 1999. 'Indo-Sri Lanka Trade and Bilateral Free Trade Agreement: A Sri Lankan Perspective', *Asia Pacific Journal*, 6(2): 87–106.

Kelegama, S. and I.N. Mukherji. 2007. 'India-Sri Lanka Bilteral Free Trade Agreement', RIS Discussion Papers No. 119, New Delhi: RIS.

Khera, R. 2011. *The Battle for Employment Guarantee.* New Delhi: Oxford University Press.

Kirk, J.A. 2008. 'Indian-Americans and the US-India Nuclear Agreement: Consolidation of an Ethnic Lobby', *Foreign Policy Analysis*, 4(3): 275–300.

Kochanek, S. 2007. 'Liberalization and Business Lobbying in India', in R. Mukherji (ed.), *India's Economic Transition.* New Delhi: Oxford University Press.

Kohli, A. 1987. *The State and Poverty in India.* New York: Cambridge University Press.

—————. 1991. *Democracy and Discontent*, pp. 315–38. New York: Cambridge University Press.

—————. 2012. *Poverty amid Plenty in the New India.* New York: Cambridge University Press.

Krasner, S.D. 1984. 'Approaches to the State', *Comparative Politics*, 16(2): 223–46.

Krishna, A. 2007. 'Politics in the Middle: Mediating Relationships Between the Citizen and the State in Rural North India', in H. Kitschelt and S.I. Wilkinson (eds), *Patrons, Clients and Policies: Patterns of Democratic Accountability and Political Competition*, pp. 141–58. New York: Cambridge University Press.

Kudaisya, M.M. 2003. *The Life and Times of G.D. Birla.* New Delhi: Oxford University Press.

Kumar, N. 2009. *India's Global Powerhouses.* Boston: Harvard Business Press.

Kumar, R. and Abhijit, S.G. 2008. 'Towards a Competitive Manufacturing Sector', Working Paper Number 203. New Delhi: Indian Council for Research on International Economic Relations.

Kux, D. 1992. *India and the United States: Estranged Democracies 1941–1991.* Washington, D.C.: National Defense University Press.

Lakshman, N. 2011. *Patrons of the Poor: Caste Politics and Policymaking in India.* New Delhi: Oxford University Press.

Lok Sabha. 1991. *Debates—July 24, 1991, 10th Series, 1–9,* pp. 271–315. New Delhi: Government of India.

Mahajan, V. 2008. 'Farmers Loan Waiver Endangers Financial Inclusion', in *India in Transition.* Philadelphia: Centre for the Advanced Study of India, University of Pennsylvania.

Majumdar, S. 2012. *India's Late, Late Industrial Revolution: Democratizing Entrepreneurship.* New York: Cambridge University Press.

Malone, D.M. 2011. *Does the Elephant Dance?* New Delhi: Oxford University Press.

Mander, H. and A. Joshi. 1998. 'The Movement for Right to Information in India', Paper presented at Pan Commonwealth Advocacy for Human Rights, Peace, and Good Governance, January. Harare: Commonwealth Human Rights Initiative.

Mansfield, E.D. and R. Bronson. 1991. 'Alliances, Preferential Trading Arrangements, and International Trade', *American Political Science Review*, 91(1): 94–107.

Mehrotra, S. and P. Lawson. 1979. 'Soviet Economic Relations with India and other Third-World Countries', *Economic and Political Weekly*, 14(30–32): 1367–92.

Mooij, J. 2001. 'Food and Power in Bihar and Jharkhand', *Economic and Political Weekly*, 36(34): 3289–99.

Muirhead, B. 2005. 'Differing Perspectives: The World Bank and the 1963 Aid India Consortium', *India Review* 4(1): 1–22.

Mukerji, S. 2007. 'State and Industrial Transformation in India', Unpublished M.Phil. Dissertation. New Delhi: Jawaharlal Nehru University.

Mukherji, I.N. 2004. 'Indo-Bangladesh Trade', *Artha Vijnana*, 46(3–4): 197–222.

Mukherji, R. 2007. 'Managing Competition', in Rahul Mukherji (ed.), *India's Economic Transition*. New Delhi: Oxford University Press, pp. 300–27.

———. 2008a. 'Promoting Foreign Investment in India's Telecommunications Sector', *Journal of Development Studies*, 44(10): 1425–45.

———. 2008b. 'Special Economic Zones in India', Institute of South Asian Studies Working Paper 30. Singapore: Institute of South Asian Studies.

———. 2008c. 'Appraising the Legacy of Bandung', in S.S. Tan and A. Acharya (eds.). *Bandung Revisited: The*

Legacy of the 1956 Asian-African Conference for International Economic Order, pp. 160–79. Singapore: NUS Press.

—————. 2009. 'Interests, Wireless Technology and Institutional Change: From Government Monopoly to Regulated Competition in Indian Telecommunications', *Journal of Asian Studies*, 68 (2): 491–517.

—————. 2010. 'Regulation and Infrastructure Development in India', in V. Chand (ed.), *Public Service Delivery in India*, pp. 177–225. New Delhi: Oxford University Press.

—————. 2010a. 'India's Foreign Economic Policies', in S. Ganguly (ed.), *India's Foreign Policy*, pp. 301–22. New Delhi: Oxford University Press.

—————. 2011. 'The Political Economy of Preferential Trade in South Asia: The Indo-Sri Lanka Free Trade Agreement', in E. Sreedharan (ed.), *International Relations Theory and South Asia Vol. 1*, pp. 301–28. New Delhi: Oxford University Press.

—————. 2013. 'Ideas, Interests and the Tipping Point: Economic Change in India', *Review of International Political Economy* 20(2): 363–89.

—————. (forthcoming). *Globalization and Deregulation: Ideas, Interests and Institutional Change in India*. New Delhi.

Mullen, R.D. and S. Ganguly. 2012. 'The Rise of India's Soft Power', *Foreign Policy*. May 8, available at http://www.foreignpolicy.com/articles/2012/05/08/the_rise_of_indian_soft_power?page=0,0 (last accessed on 28 May 2012).

Murgai, R. 2007. 'Teacher Compensation', *India Policy Forum 2006/07*, pp. 123–78. Washington, D.C. and New Delhi: Brookings Institution and Sage.

Nair, M. 2011. 'Differences in Workers' Narratives of Contention in Two Central Indian Towns', *International Labor and Working-Class History*, 79(1): 175–94.

Narasimhan, M. (Chair). 1985. *Report of the Committee to Examine Principles of a Possible Shift Physical to Financial Controls.* New Delhi: Ministry of Finance.

Narayana Murthy, N.R. 2011. 'India Inc.', in M.M. Kudaisya (ed.), *The Oxford India Anthology of Business History*, pp. 462–72. New Delhi: Oxford University Press.

Nayar, B.R. 1977. 'India and the Super Powers', *Economic and Political Weekly*, 14(30): 1185–89.

—————. 1989. *India's Mixed Economy.* Bombay: Popular Prakashan.

—————. (ed.). 2007. *Globalization and Politics in India.* New Delhi: Oxford University Press.

—————. 2006. 'When Did the Hindu Rate of Growth End?' *Economic and Political Weekly*, 13 May. pp. 1885–90.

—————. 2007. 'The Limits of Economic Nationalism in India', in Rahul Mukherji (ed.), *India's Economic Transition*, pp. 202–30. New Delhi: Oxford University Press.

Nooruddin, I. 2011. *Coalition Politics and Economic Development.* New York: Cambridge University Press.

Pai, S. 2010. *Developmental State and the Dalit Question in Madhya Pradesh: Congress Response.* New Delhi: Routledge.

Panagariya, A. 2008. *India: The Emerging Giant*. New Delhi: Oxford University Press.

Patel, I.G. 2003. *Glimpses of Indian Economic Policies*. New Delhi: Oxford University Press.

Pederson, J.D. 2000. 'Explaining Economic Liberalization in India', *World Development*, 28(2): 265–82.

Pierson, P. 2004. *Politics in Time*. Princeton: Princeton University Press.

Pingle, V. 2000. *Rethinking the Developmental State*. New Delhi: Oxford University Press.

Pohit, S. and N. Taneja. 2003. 'India's Informal Trade with Bangladesh', *The World Economy*, 26(8): 1187–1214.

Reddy, D.N. 2013. 'Functioning of NREGS in Andhra Pradesh', in K.P. Kannan and J. Breman (eds). *The Long Road to Social Security*, pp. 117–63. New Delhi: Oxford University Press.

Roy, A., N. Dey, and S. Pande. 2008. 'The Right to Information Act 2005: A Development Perspective', in H.M. Mathur (ed.), *India: Social Development Report–2008*, pp. 205–20. New Delhi: Council for Social Development and Oxford University Press.

Roy Chowdhury, S. 2007. 'Public Sector Restructuring and Democracy', in R. Mukherji (ed.), *India's Economic Transition*, pp. 338–411. New Delhi: Oxford University Press.

Rudolph, L.I. 1979. 'Comment', in J.W. Mellor and P. Talbot (eds), *India: A Rising Middle Power*, pp. 69–76. Colorado: Westview.

Rudolph, L.I. and Susanne H.R. 2007. 'Iconization of Chandrababu: Sharing Sovereignty in India's Federal Market Economy', in R. Mukherji, (ed.), *India's Economic Transition*, pp. 231–64. New Delhi: Oxford University Press.

—————. 2012. 'The Political Role of India's Caste Associations', *Pacific Affairs*, 85(2): 335–53.

Ruparelia, S., S. Reddy, J. Harriss, and S. Corbridge (eds). 2011. *Understanding India's New Political Economy: A Great Transformation?* New York: Routledge.

Sahni, V. 2006. 'Limited Cooperation Between Limited Allies: India's Strategic Programs and the India–US Strategic Trade', in S. Ganguly, B. Shuop, and A. Scobel. (eds), *US–Indian Strategic Cooperation: Into the 21st Century*, pp. 173–91. London: Routledge.

Sardesai, D.R. 1964. *Indian Foreign Policy in Cambodia, Laos and Vietnam.* Berkeley: University of California Press.

Saxenian, AnnaLee. 2007. 'Bangalore: The Silicon Valley of Asia', in Rahul Mukherji (ed.), *India's Economic Transition*, pp. 359–87. New Delhi: Oxford University Press.

Sen, A. 1998. 'Theory and Practice of Development', in I.J. Ahluwalia and I.M.D. Little (eds), *India's Economic Reforms and Development: Essays for Manmohan Singh*, pp. 73–84. New Delhi: Oxford University Press.

Shankar, S., R. Gaiha, and R. Jha. 2011. 'Information Access and Targeting: The National Rural Employment Guarantee Scheme in India', *Oxford Development Studies*, 39(1): 69–95.

Shastri, V. 1995. 'The Political Economy of Policy Reform in India', Unpublished PhD Dissertation, pp. 223–6. New York: Cornell University.

Singh, M. 1964. *India's Export Trends and Prospects for Self-sustained Growth*. Oxford: Clarendon Press.

Singh, S.N. 1986. *The Yogi and the Bear*. London: Mansell Publishing Limited.

Singh, S. 2010. 'The Genesis and Evolution of the Right to Information Regime in India', Paper presented at Workshop: Towards More Open and Transparent Governance in South Asia. New Delhi, 27–29 April.

Sinha, A. 2005. 'Divided Leviathan: The Regional Roots of Developmental Politics in India'. New Delhi: Oxford University Press.

———. 2005. 'Understanding the Rise and Transformation of Business Collective Action in India', *Business and Politics*, 7(2): 1–27.

———. 2007. 'Global Linkages and Domestic Politics: Trade Reform and Institutional Building in India in a Comparative Perspective', *Comparative Political Studies*, 40(10): 1183–1210.

Sridharan, E. 1993. 'Economic Liberalization and India's Political Economy: Towards a Paradigm Synthesis', *Journal of Commonwealth and Comparative Politics*, 31(3): 1–31.

Sridharan, K. 1996. *The ASEAN Region in India's Foreign Policy*. Aldershot: Dartmouth Publishing.

Stepan, A., J.J. Linz and Y. Yadav. 2011. *Crafting State Nations: India and other Multinational Democracies*. Baltimore: Johns Hopkins University Press.

Subramanian, N. 1999. *Ethnicity and Populist Mobilization: Political Parties, Citizenship and Democracy in South India*. New Delhi: Oxford University Press.

Tendulkar, S.D. and T.A. Bhavani. 2007. *Understanding Reforms*. New Delhi: Oxford University Press.

Thachil, T. 2011. 'Embedded Mobilization: Nonstate Service Provision as Electoral Strategy in India', *World Politics*, 63(3): 434–69.

Thakur, R. 1994. *The Politics and Economics of India's Foreign Policy*. London: Hurst and Company.

Tilly, C. 1992. *Coercion, Capital and European States: AD 1990–1992*. Maiden, Massachusetts: Wiley Blackwell.

Tongia, R. 2007. 'The Political Economy of Indian Power Sector Reforms', in D.G. Victor and T.C. Heller (eds). *The Political Economy of Power Sector Reform*, pp. 109–74. Cambridge: Cambridge University Press.

Varshney, A. 1998. *Democracy, Development and the Countryside*. New York: Cambridge University Press.

————. 2000. 'Is India Becoming More Democratic?', *Journal of Asian Studies*, 59(1): 3–25.

————. 2007. 'Mass Politics and Elite Politics', in R. Mukherji (ed.), *India's Economic Transition*, pp. 146–69. New Delhi: Oxford University Press.

Venkatsubramanian, A.K. 2006. 'The Political Economy of the Public Distribution System in Tamil Nadu', in

V. Chand (ed), *Reinventing Public Service Delivery in India*, pp. 266–93. Washington and New Delhi: The World Bank and Sage.

Vickery, R.E. 2011. *Strategic Aspects of US-India Economic Engagement*. New Delhi: Oxford University Press.

Wade, R. 1990. *Governing the Market*. Princeton: Princeton University Press.

Walton, M. 2009. 'The Political Economy of India's Malnutrition Puzzle', *IDS Bulletin*, 40(4): 16–24.

Weerakoon, D. 2010. 'The Political Economy of Trade Integration in South Asia', *The World Economy*, 33(7): 916–27.

Weiner, M. 1979. 'Assessing the Impact of Foreign Assistance', in J.W. Mellor and Philips Talbot (eds), *India and Rising Middle Power*, pp. 49–68. Colorado: Westview Press.

—————. 1990. *The Child and the State in India: Child Labor and Education Policy in Comparative Perspective*, Princeton: Princeton University Press.

Yadav, Y. and S. Palshikar. 2009. 'Between Fortuna and Virtu: Explaining the Congress's Ambiguous Victory in 2009', *Economic and Political Weekly*, 44(39): 33–46.

Index